CW01638757

# NEWMANSHIP

Nicholas Newman

ADLARD COLES LIMITED
8 Grafton Street, London W1

Adlard Coles Ltd
William Collins Sons & Co. Ltd
8 Grafton Street, London W1X 3LA

First published in Great Britain by
Adlard Coles Ltd 1985

Distributed in the United States of America
by Sheridan House, Inc.



*British Library Cataloguing in Publication Data*
Newman, Nicholas
Newmanship : the sailing scene observed.
1. English wit and humor, Pictorial
I. Title
741.5'942 NC1479

ISBN 0-229-11753-8

Typeset by Columns of Reading
Printed and bound in Great Britain by
Mackays of Chatham Ltd, Kent

If you were inspired by Thor Heyerdahl's epic expedition in the *Ra*, or moved by Tim Severin's bold imitation of St Brendan's Atlantic voyage, then this book is unlikely to assume a place of pride and prominence in your library. If, however, your literary hunger is for something to put between the pot plant and the airfreshener in your loo, then this slender tome may just fill the gap. It does not seek to prove that the Egyptians visited Mexico, that an Irish monk discovered America or that the Polynesians invented Travel Scrabble. If there is a central thesis, it is only that sailing is a rather eccentric pastime, which can make you very cold and wet on a Sunday afternoon; and that this is probably more easily achieved by sitting in a bucket of water in the fridge. For this amazing conclusion, I must thank my father, and for the publication of my theorem, the editors of *Yachting Monthly* and the late *Offshore Sailing*, who have been extraordinarily indulgent in encouraging my ideas – most of which first appeared in their pages.

Nicholas Newman

# SEAMANSHIP

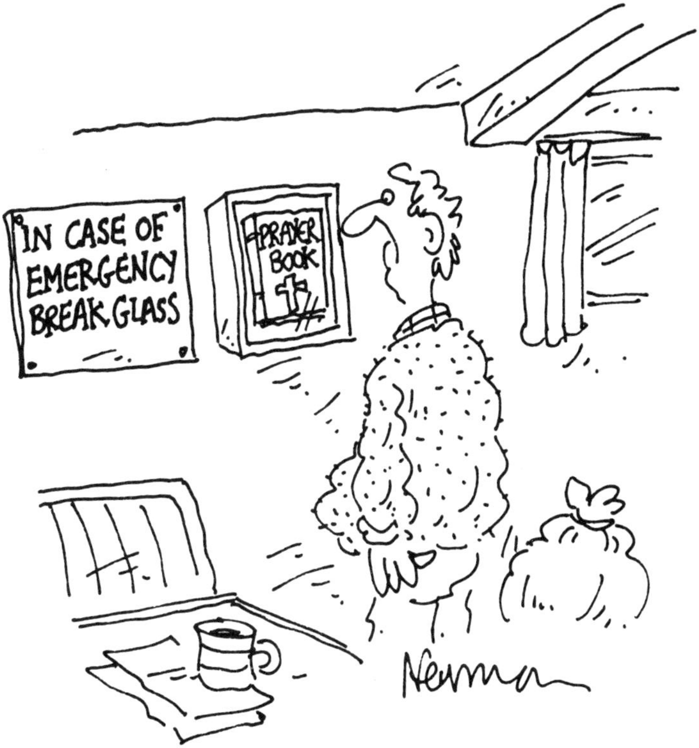

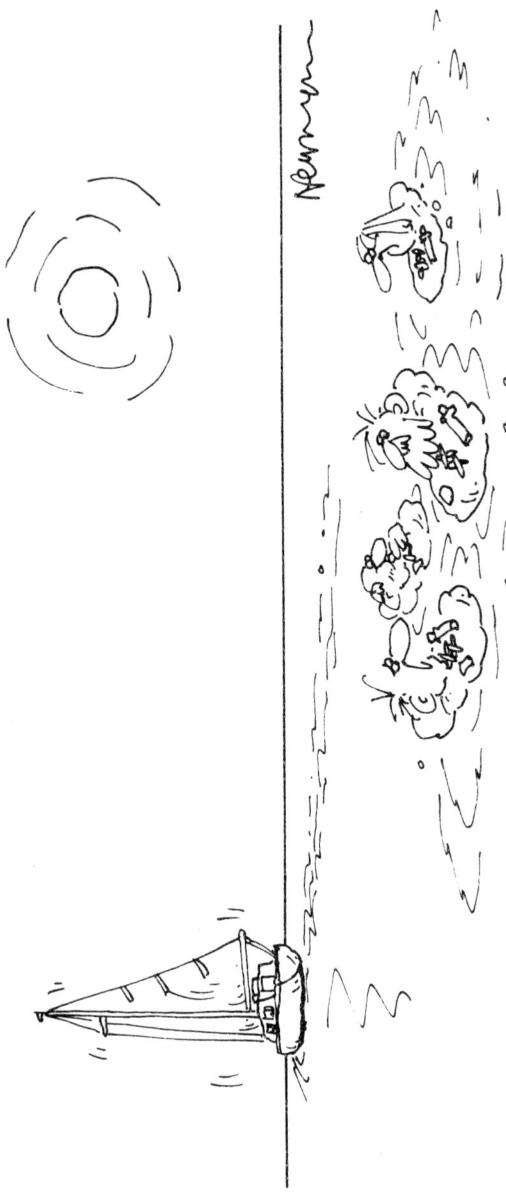

'Well, so much for the fire drill!'

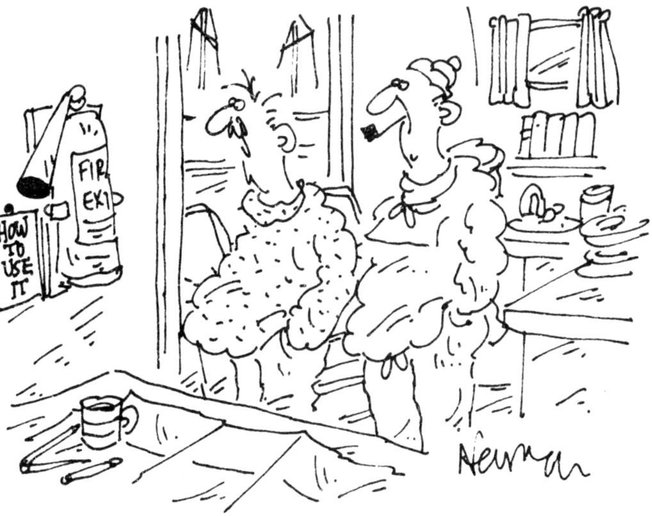


*'It was so expensive that if we had a fire, it'd be difficult to decide between the extinguisher and the boat.'*

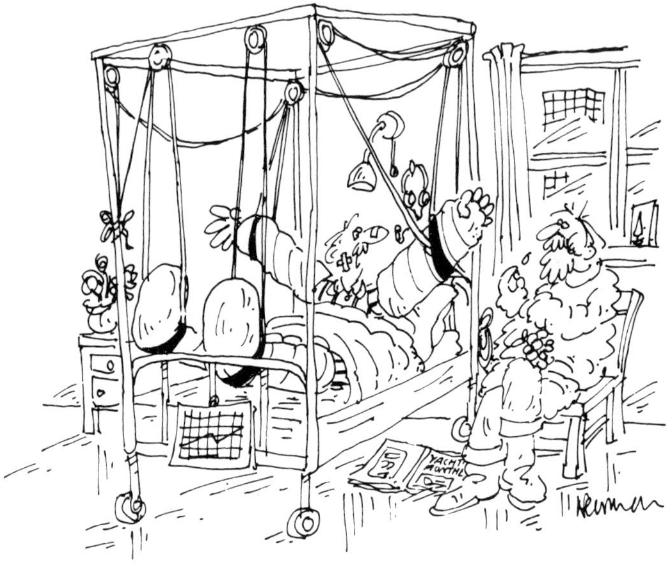


*'Silly, really; I tripped up on some safety gear.'*

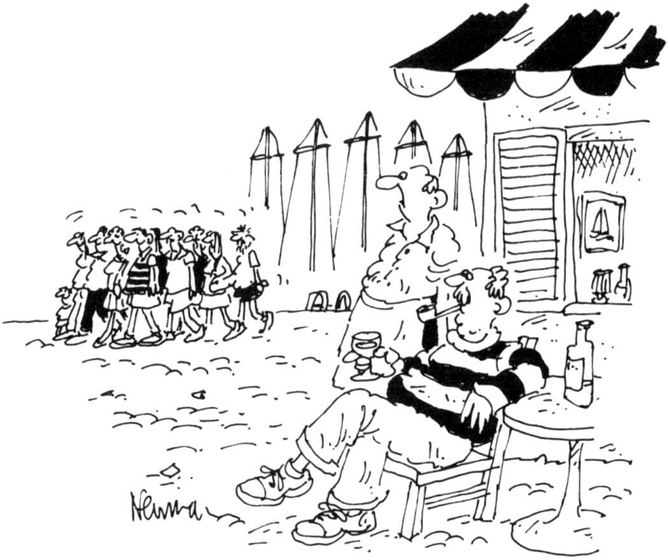

*'You can always spot the flotilla sailors.'*

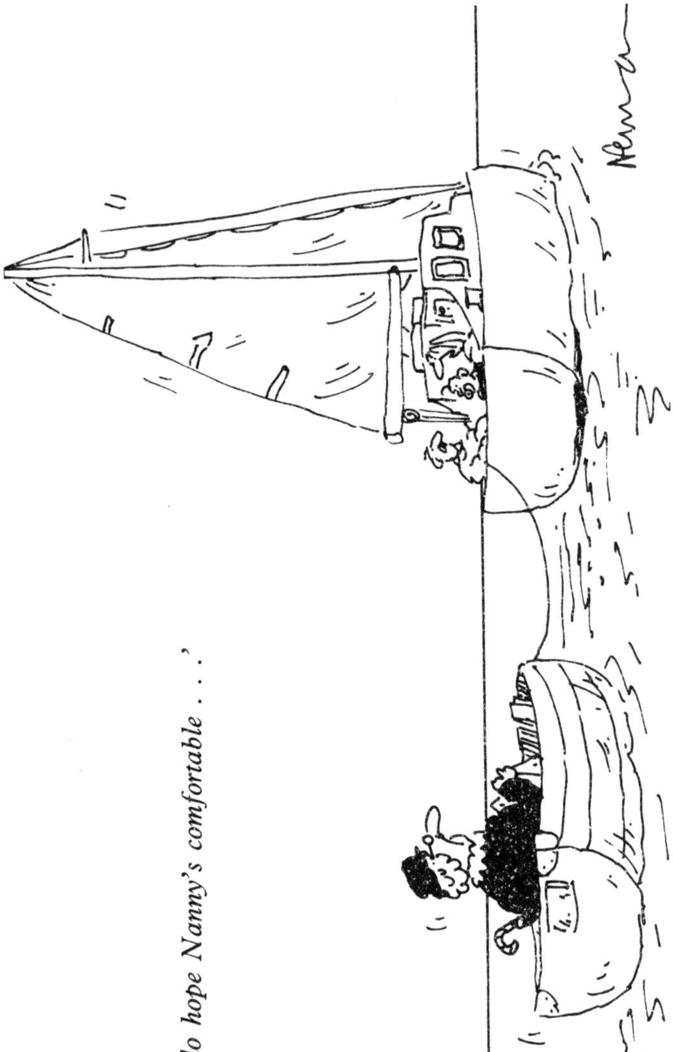

'I do hope Nanny's comfortable . . .'

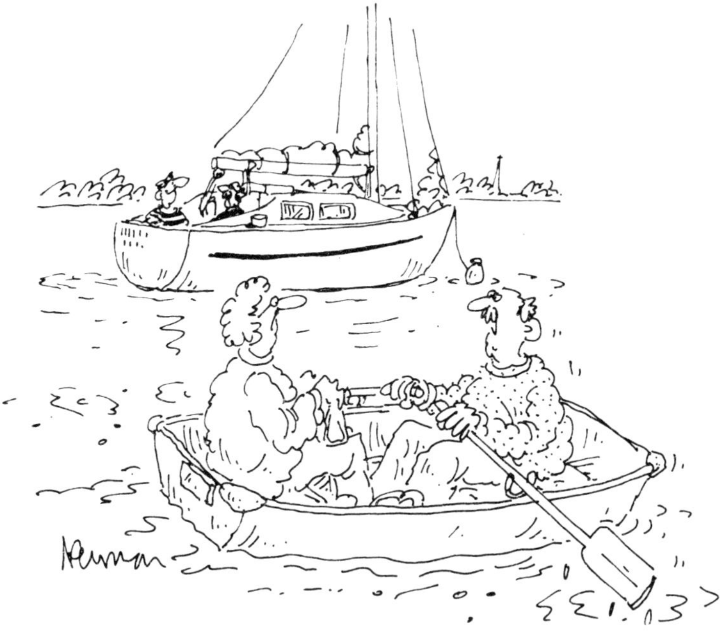

*'It's the ultimate safety precaution. He only goes sailing with his life insurance salesman.'*

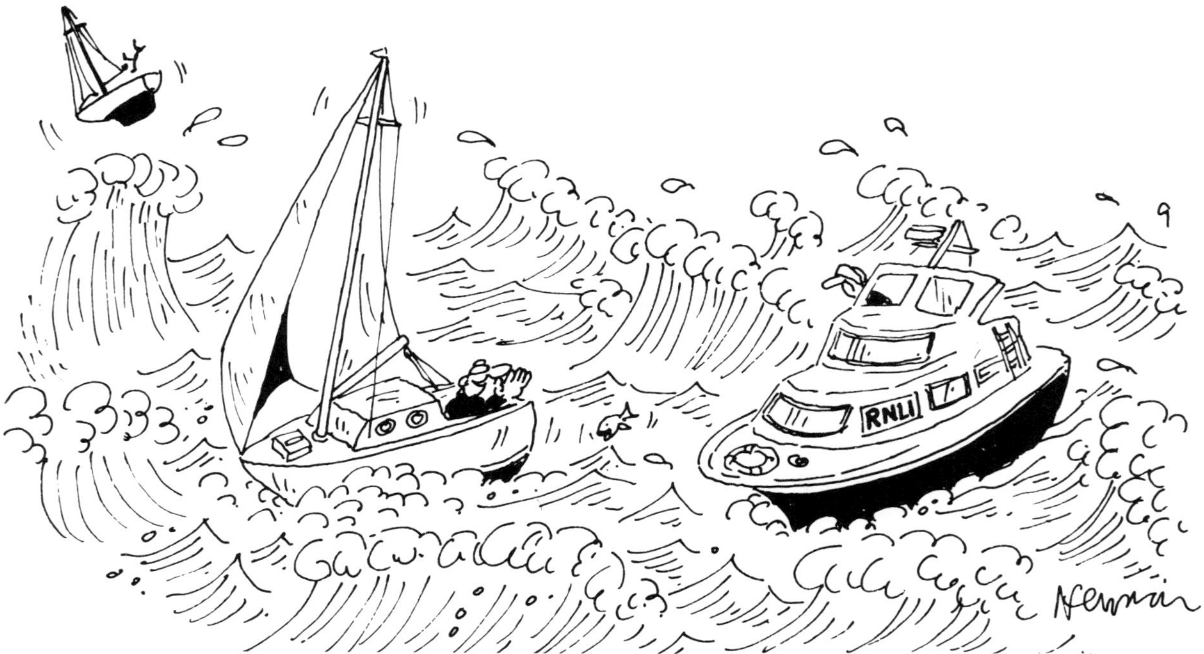


*'I suppose I'm a bit of a safety nut – I only ever go sailing when the lifeboat's out!'*

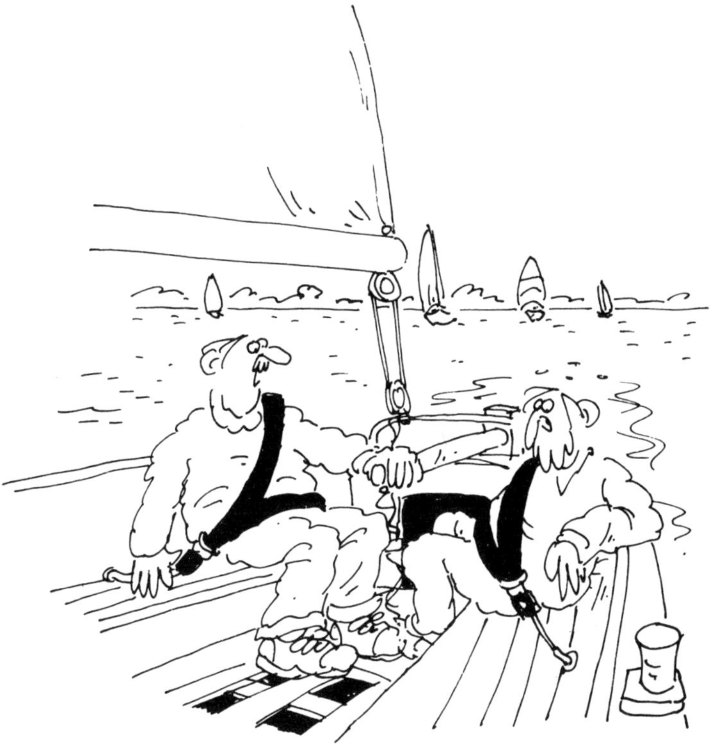

*'She has a tendency to broach rather suddenly.'*

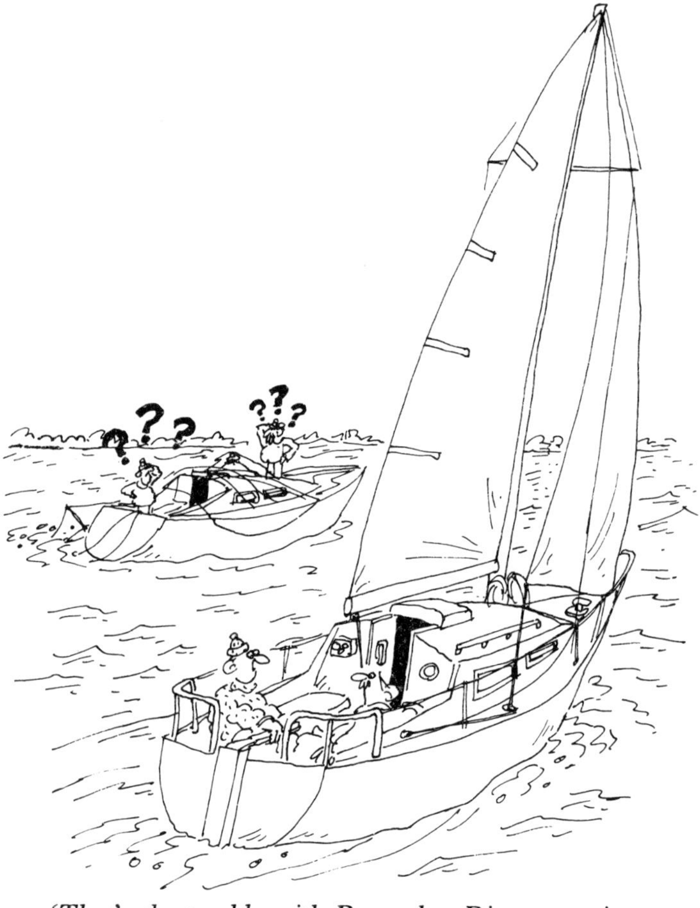


*'That's the trouble with Bermudan Rig – sometimes it just vanishes without trace.'*

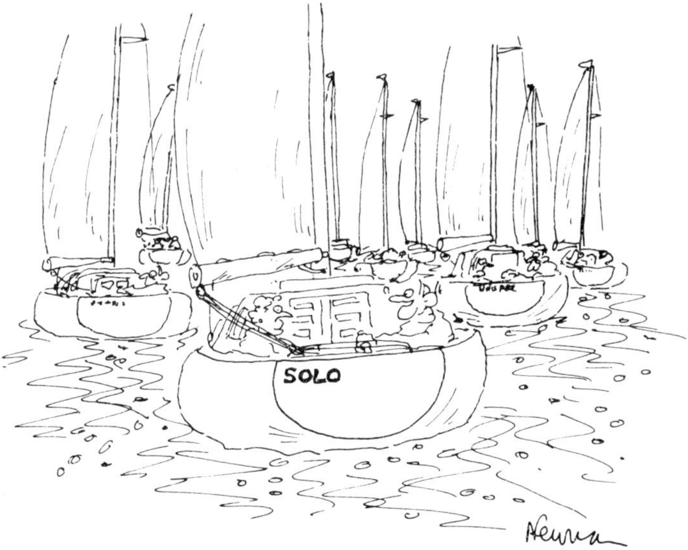


*'There's nothing quite like an ocean cruise for getting away from it all . . .'*

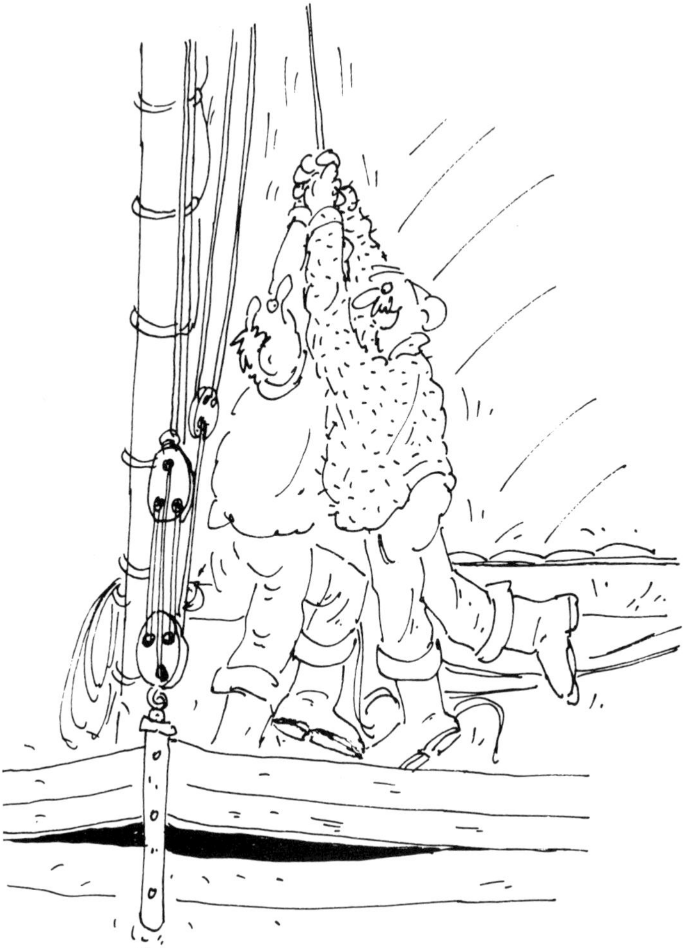

*'Tailing the throat onto your shroud lanyards is the authentic way to set up your rigging – HEAVE!'*

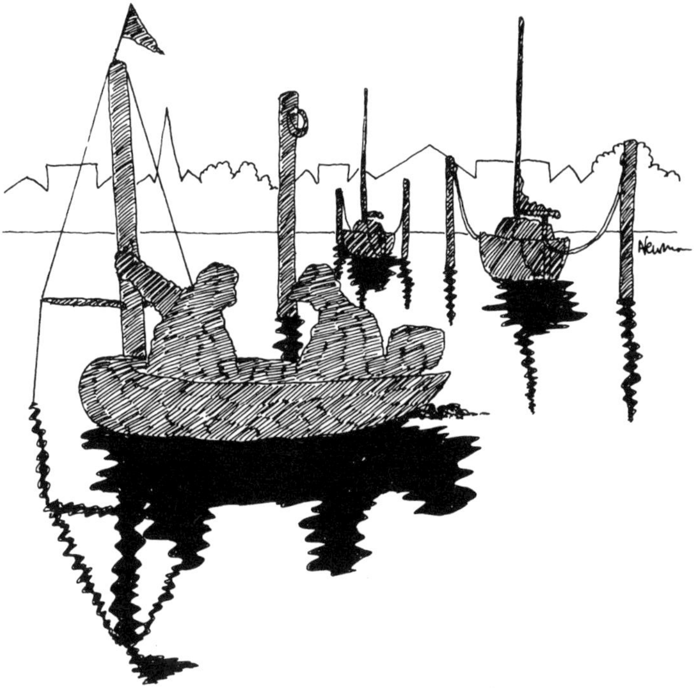

*'I vote we panic . . .'*

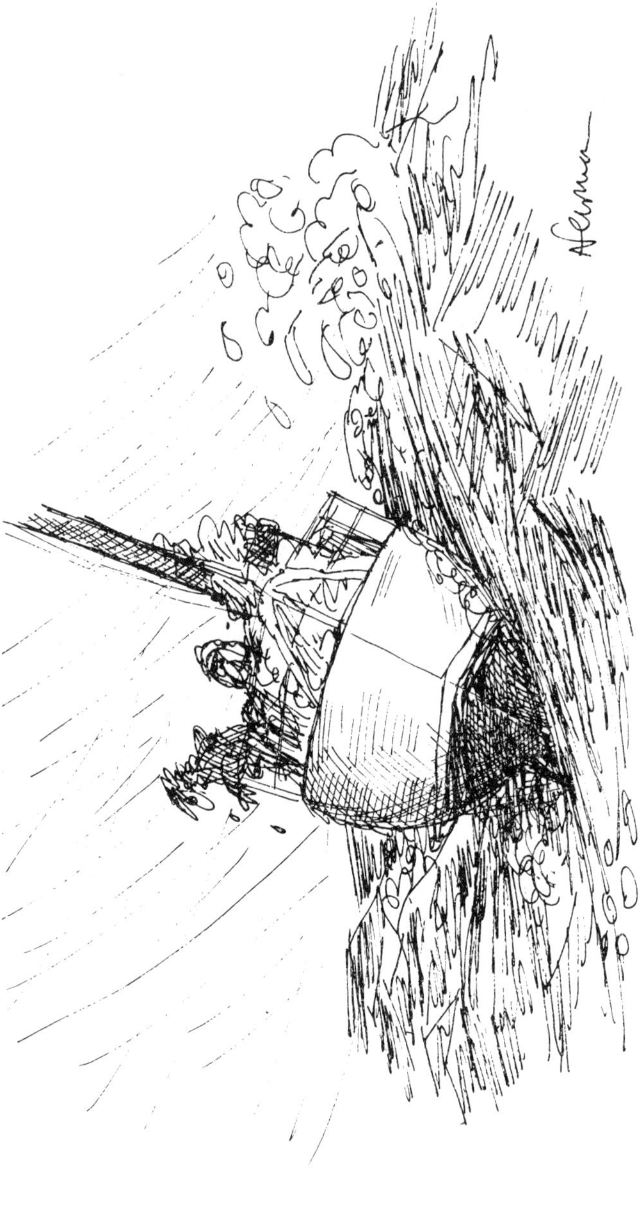

'Downwind *next time, if you don't mind . . .*'

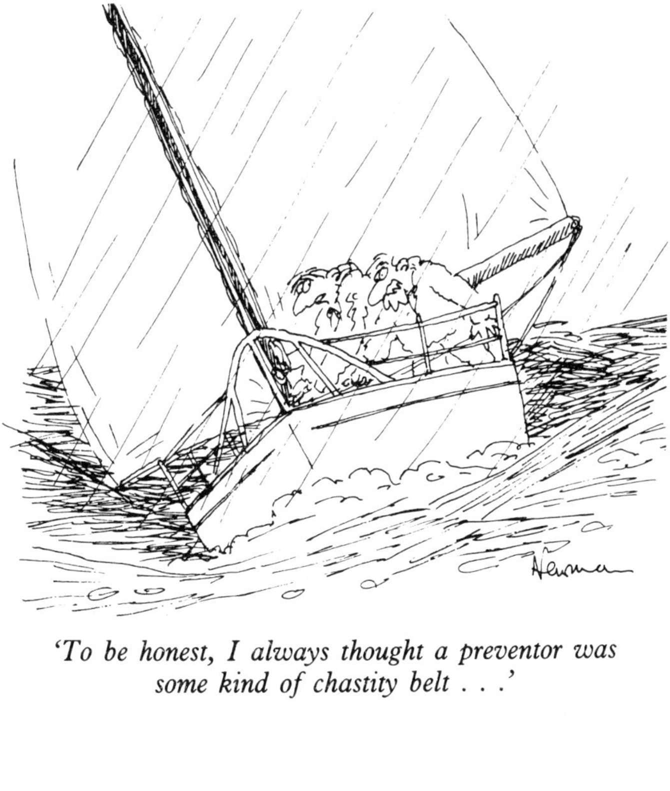


*'To be honest, I always thought a preventor was some kind of chastity belt . . .'*

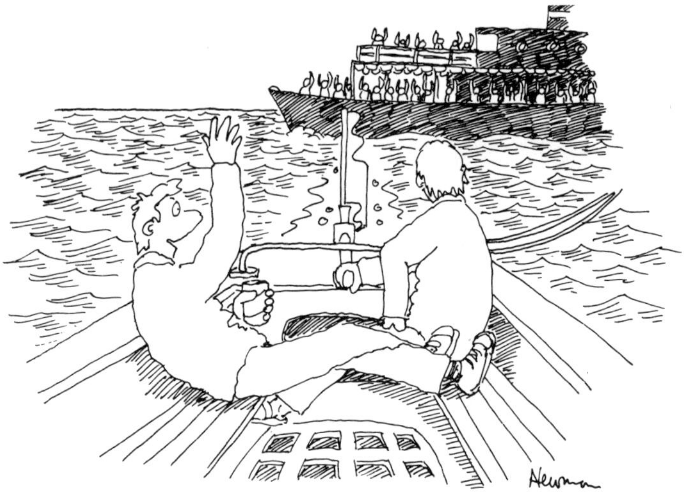

*'Hands up all those who are wearing grubby vests . . .'*

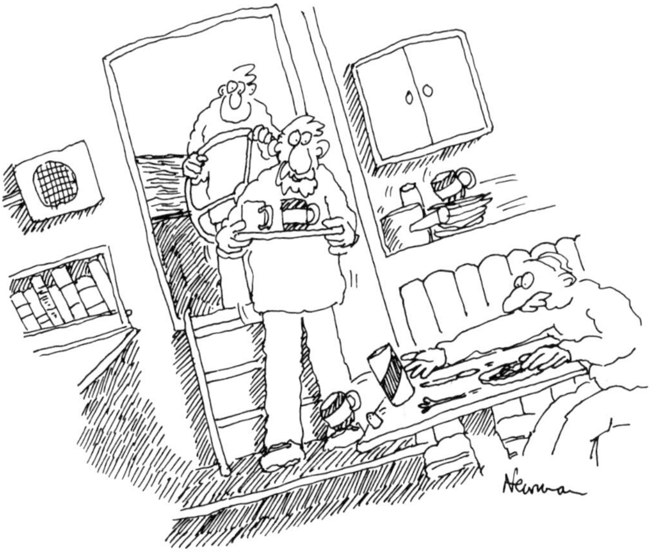

*'Thank God the Almighty had the foresight to make man gimbaled . . .'*

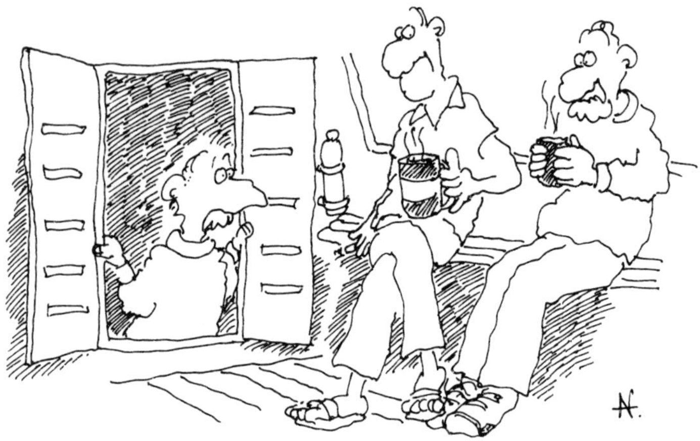

*'It* was *diesel in the port tank and water in the starboard wasn't it?'*

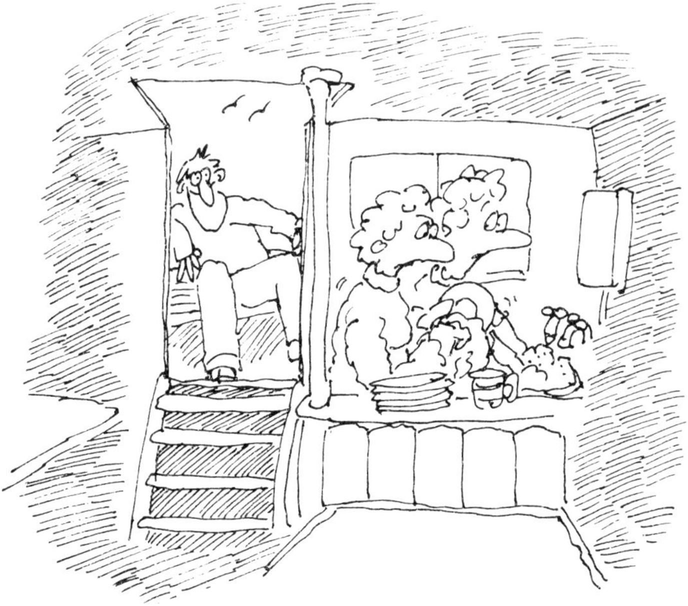

*'I think it's the sea, the sun, the fresh air and the exercise that* really *attract me to sailing . . .'*

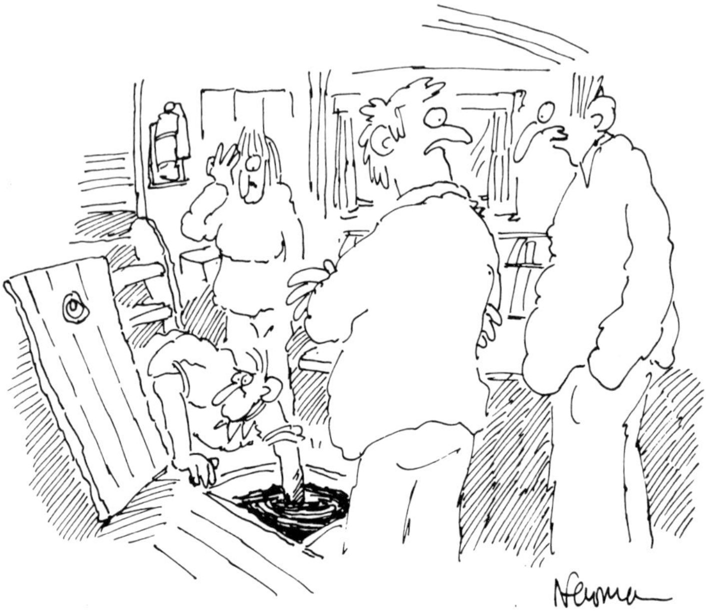

*'If it was* my *contact lens, I'm not altogether sure that I'd* want *him to find it . . .'*

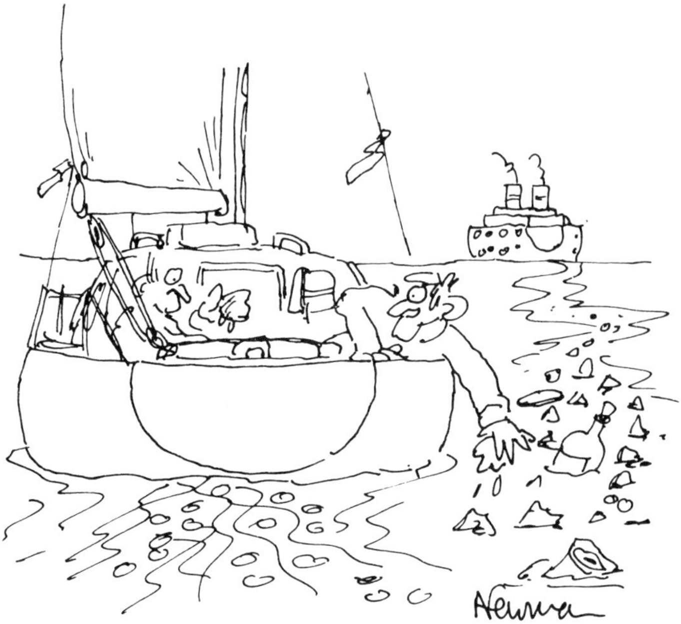

*'It really is excellent quality – it just needs to be réchaufféd . . .'*

# SHOREMANSHIP

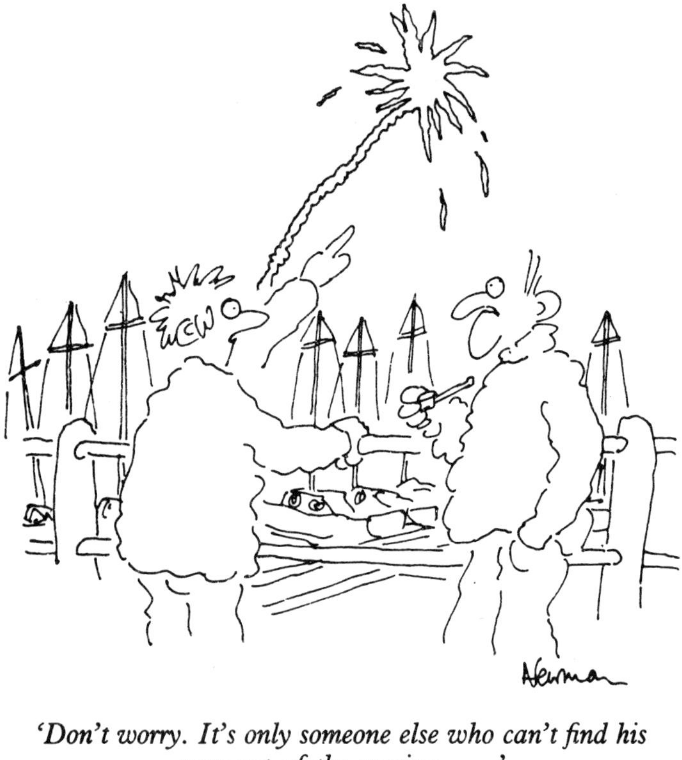


*'Don't worry. It's only someone else who can't find his way out of the marina . . .'*

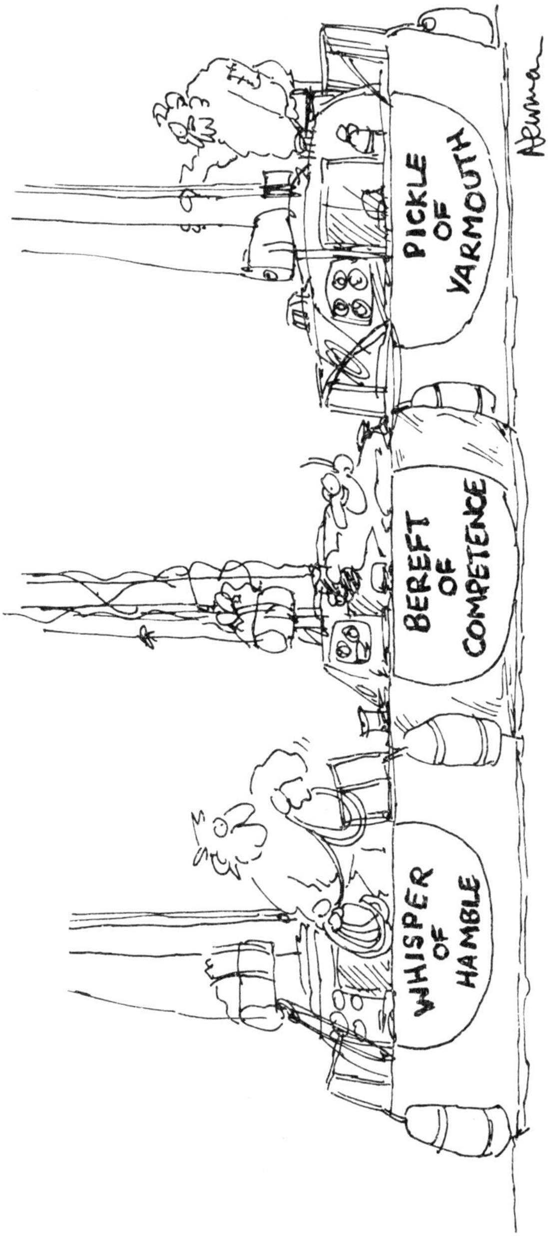
PICKLE OF YARMOUTH
BEREFT OF COMPETENCE
WHISPER OF HAMBLE

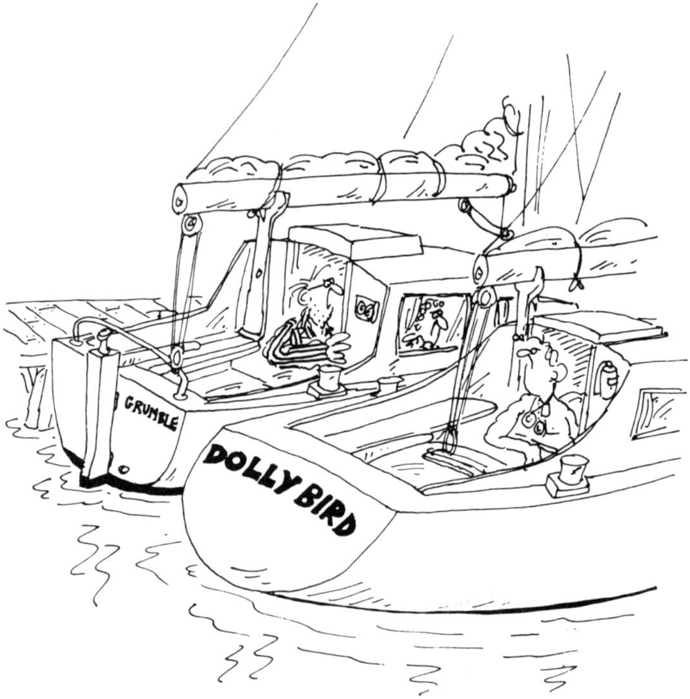


*'I don't mind your tapping halyard — it's your bloody jangling medallions that I can't stand!'*

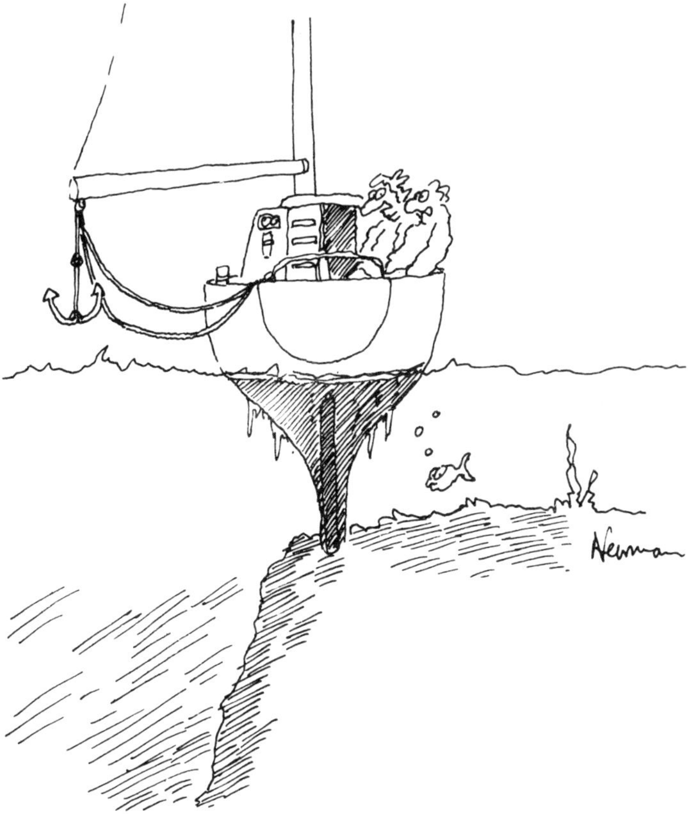

*'. . . no problem really – she lies at about 30° when she dries out, and refloats very comfortably . . .'*

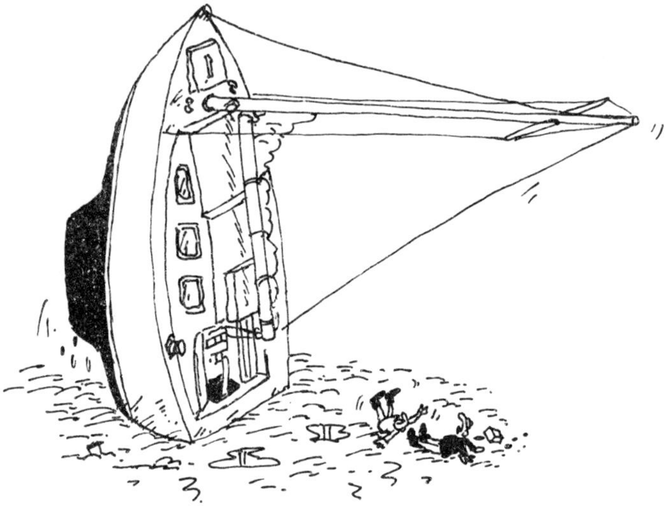

*'By God, this mud's slippery!'*

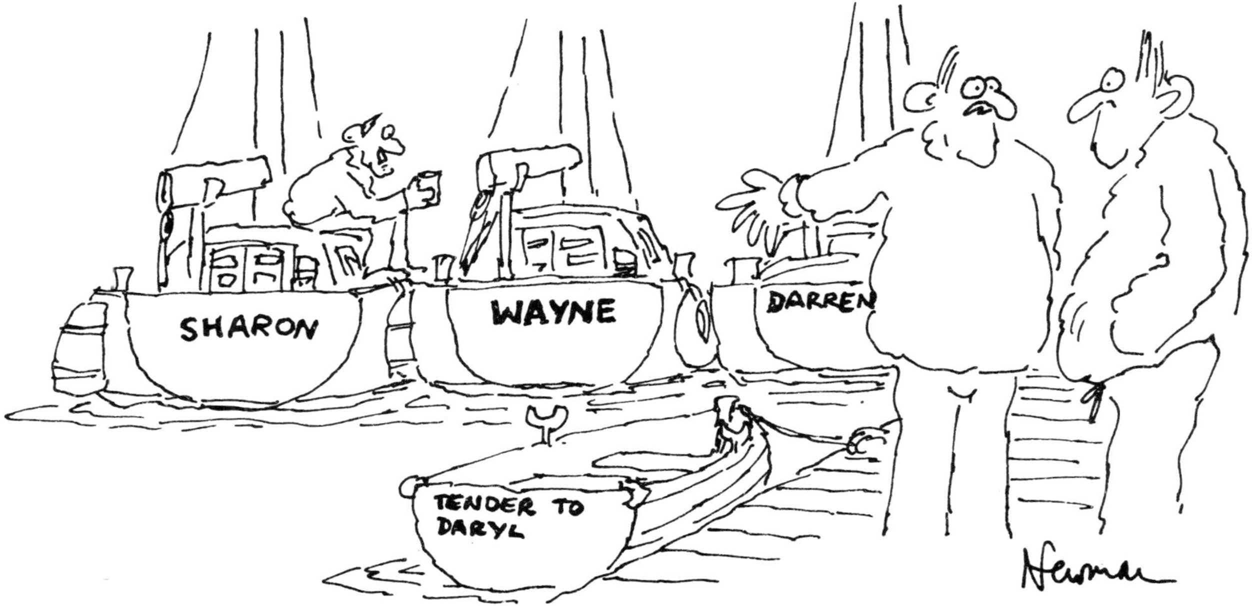


*'This is the more downmarket end of the marina . . .'*

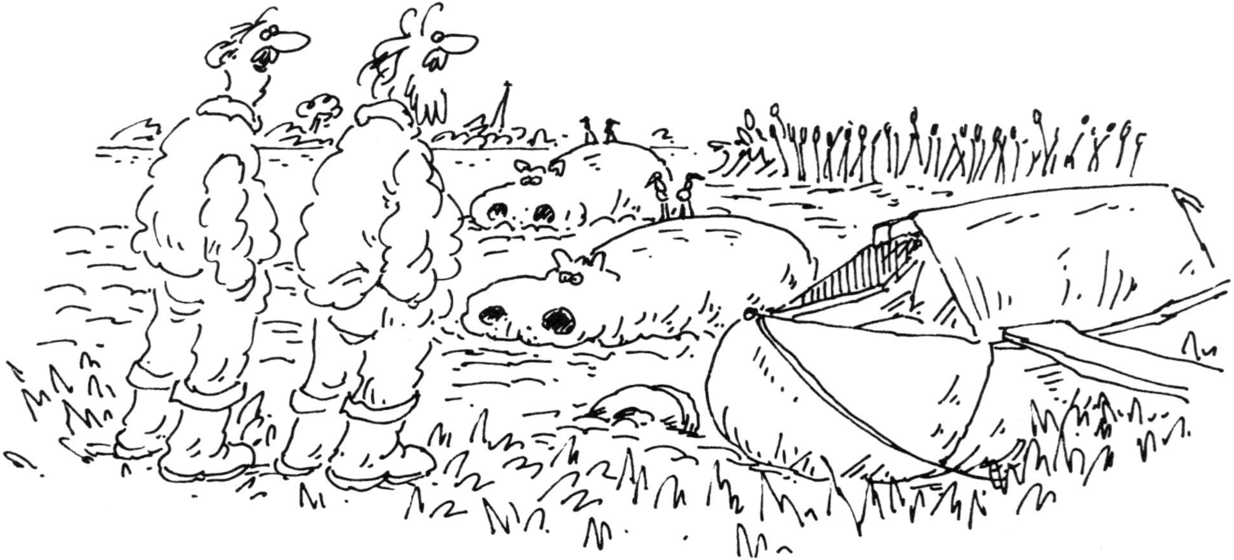

'The mud berths here are renowned for being some of the best in the world.'

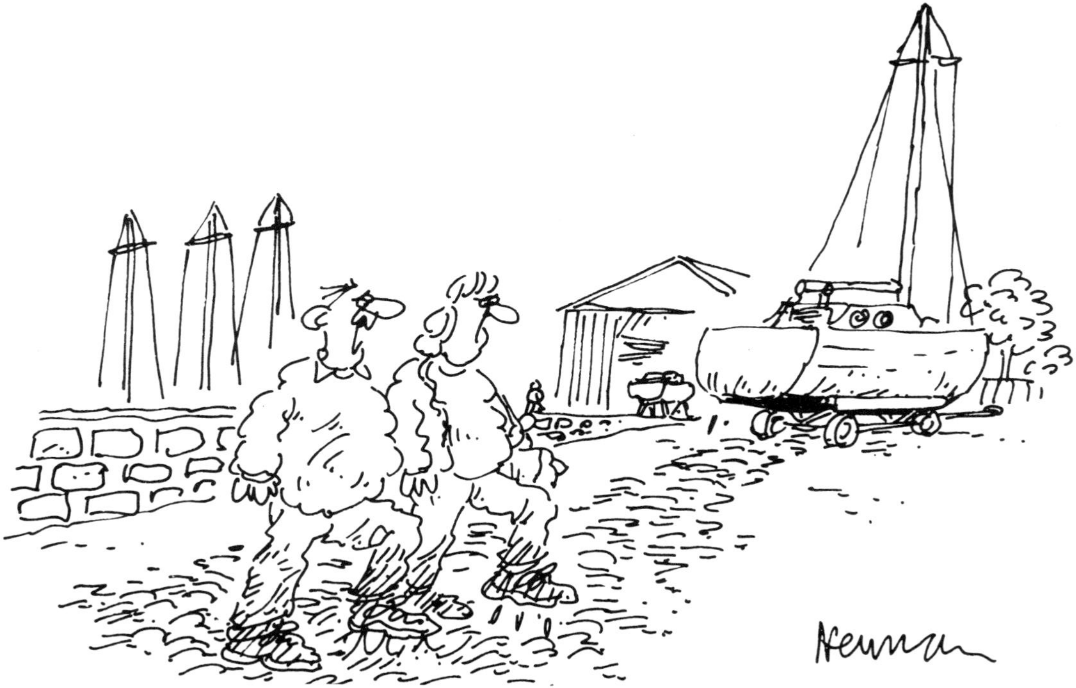

*'I wish people would wipe their boats before coming ashore!'*

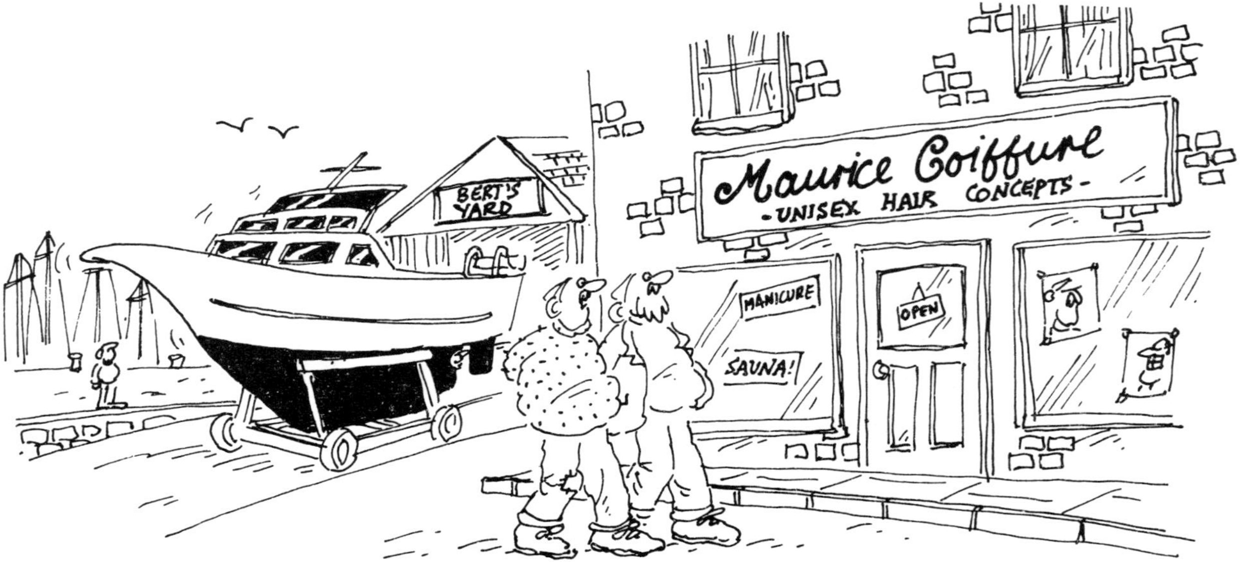


'. . . and that's where they're refitting the crew.'

# WORKMANSHIP

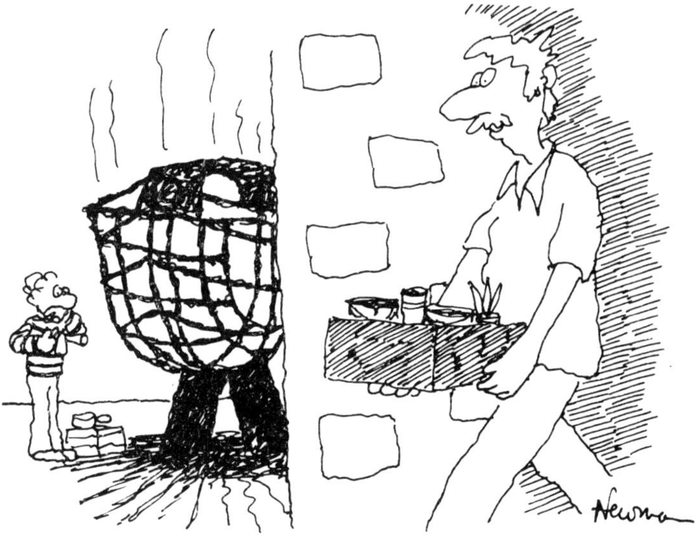

*'How are we getting on with the burner then?'*

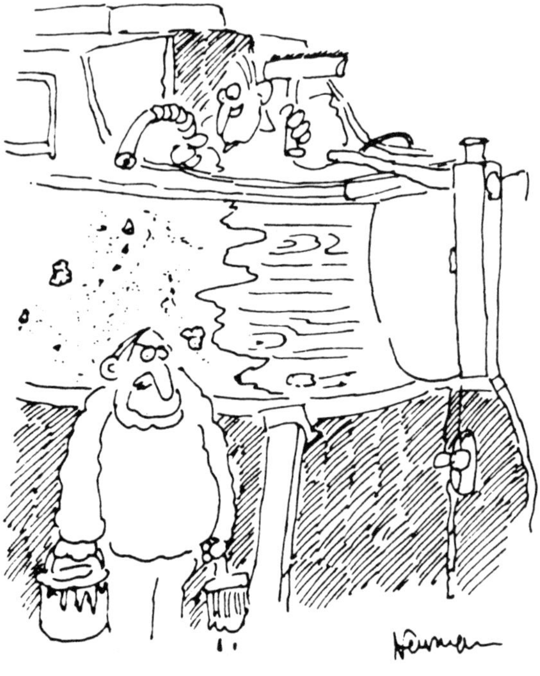

*'I've discovered why the vacuum cleaner wasn't sucking properly . . .'*

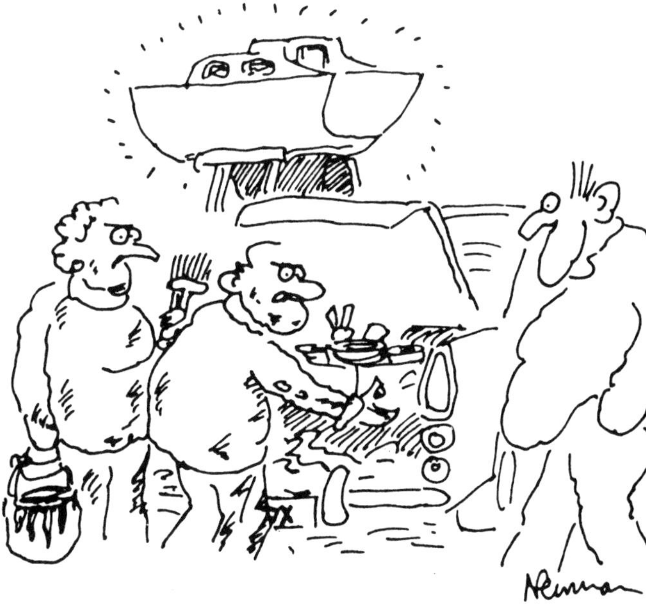

*'Just starting, eh?'*

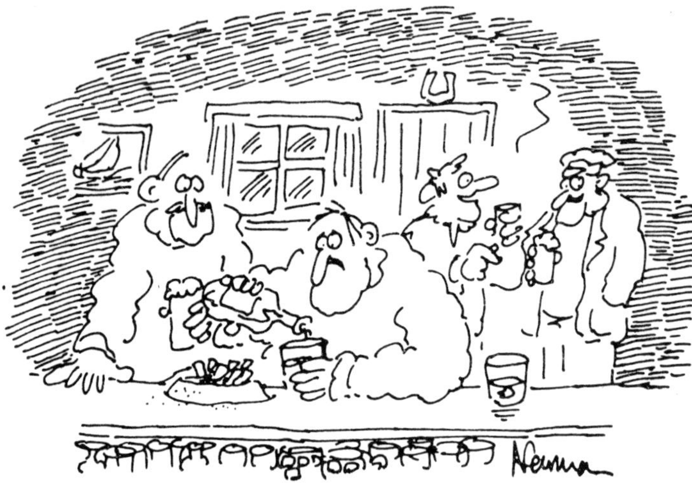

*'I've got to sell the boat to pay for the damn antifouling . . .'*

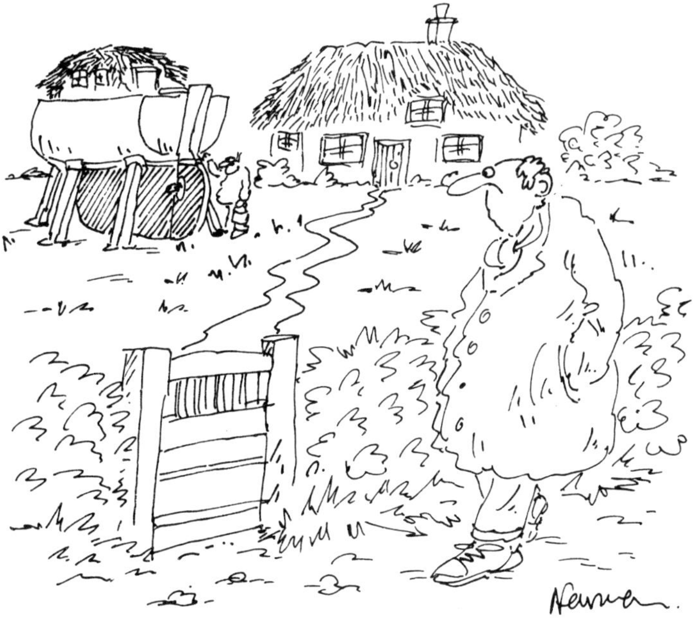

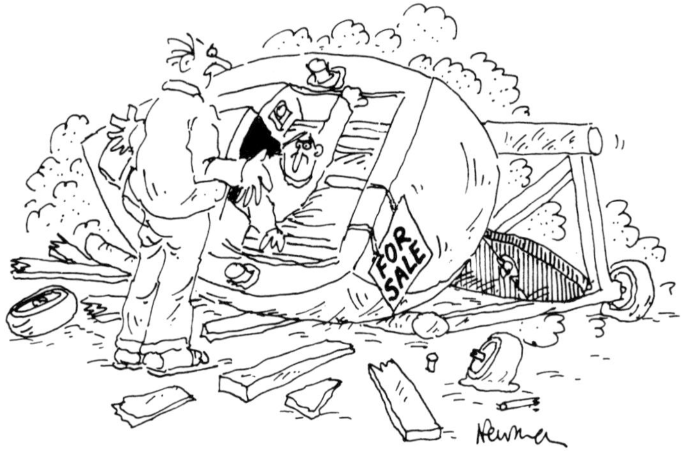


*'All I did was kick the damn tyre . . .'*

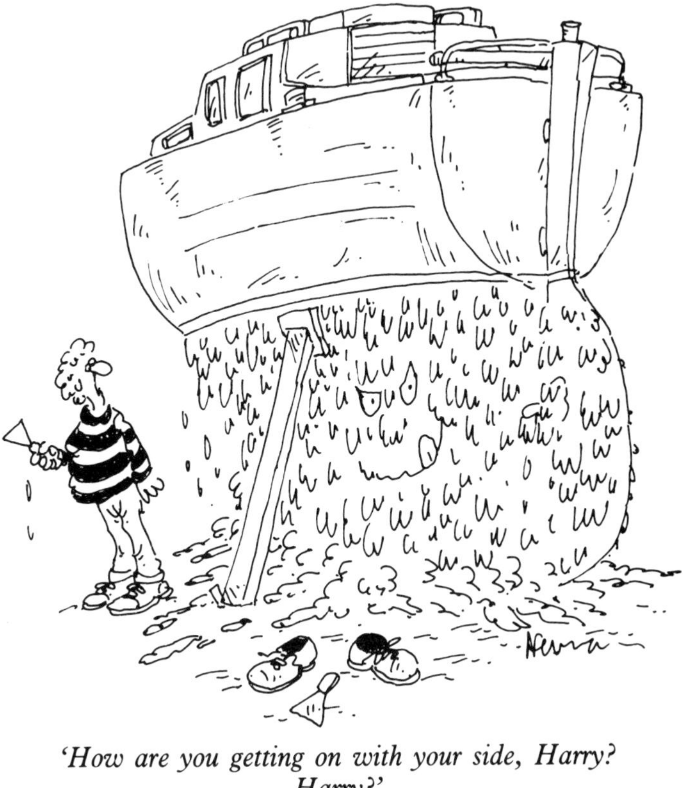

*'How are you getting on with your side, Harry? Harry?'*

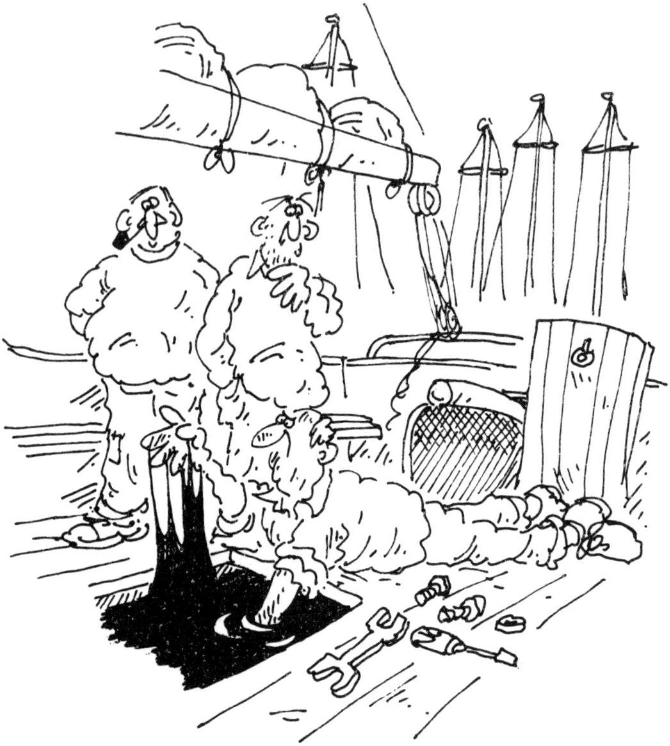

*'I could have sworn the engine was down there somewhere . . .'*

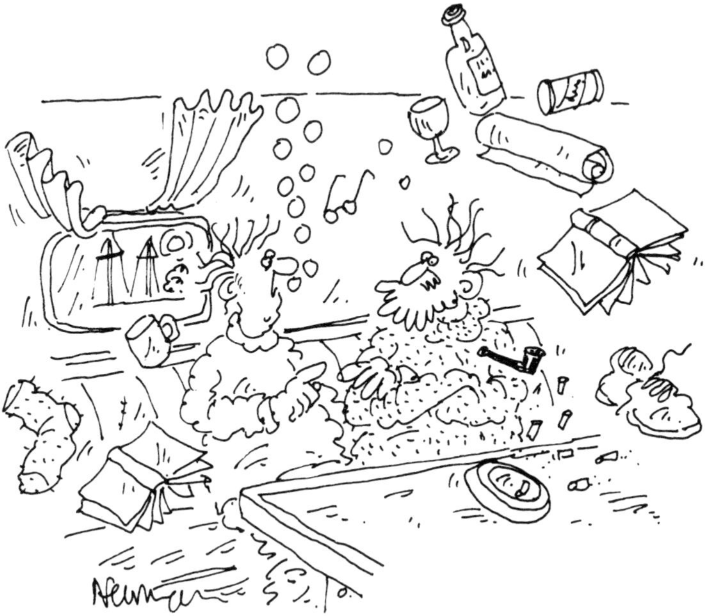

*'Has winter condensation always been such a problem?*

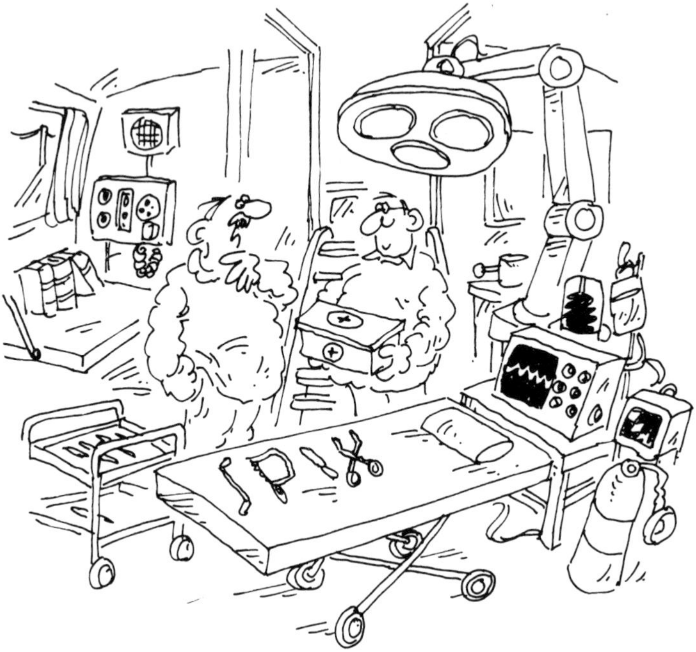

*'I must confess, as first aid boxes go it's pretty impressive.'*

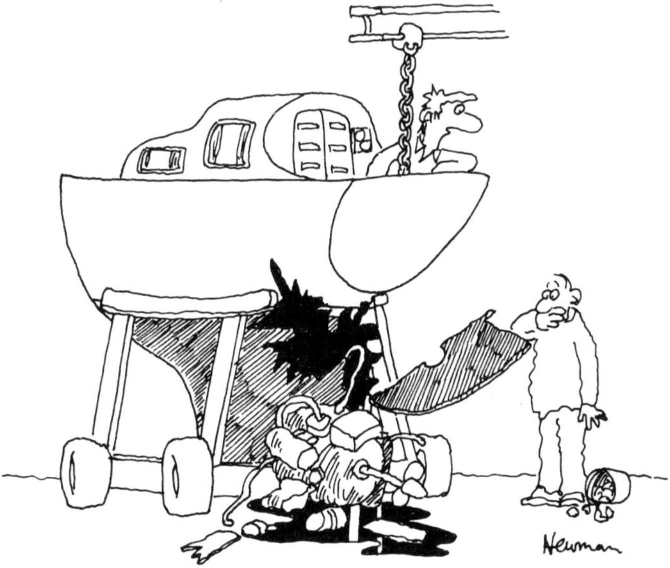


*'You were quite right guv'nor – the 50 horsepower was* too big *. . .'*

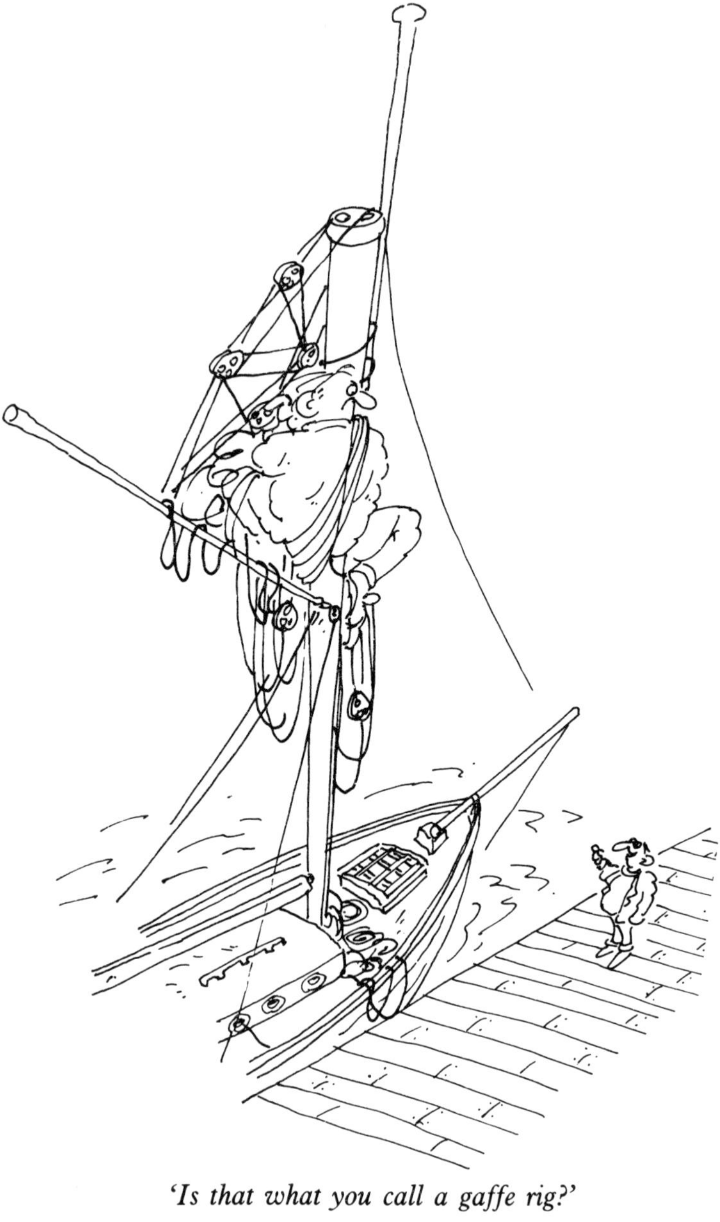

*'Is that what you call a gaffe rig?'*

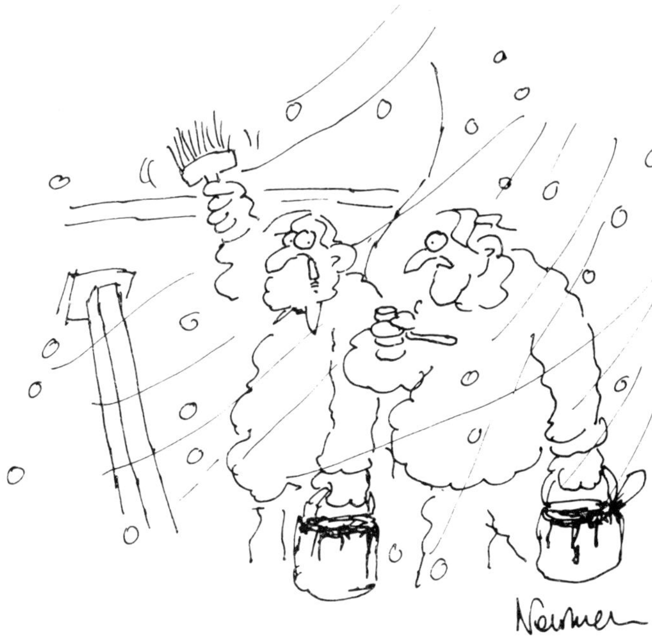


*'How many New Year's resolutions are* you *breaking?'*

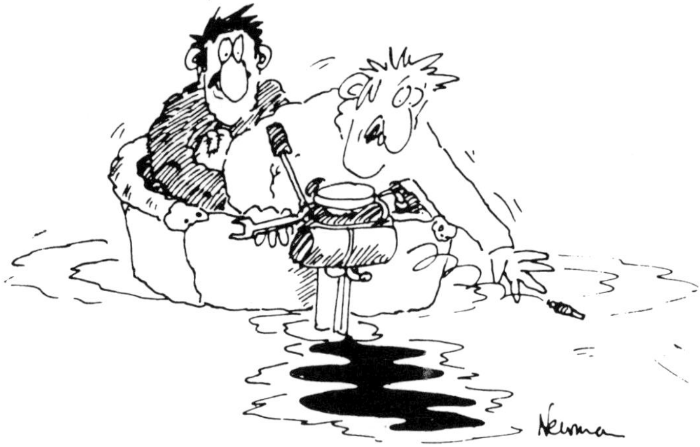

*'Well, it could be worse – you could have dropped the spark plug overboard . . .'*

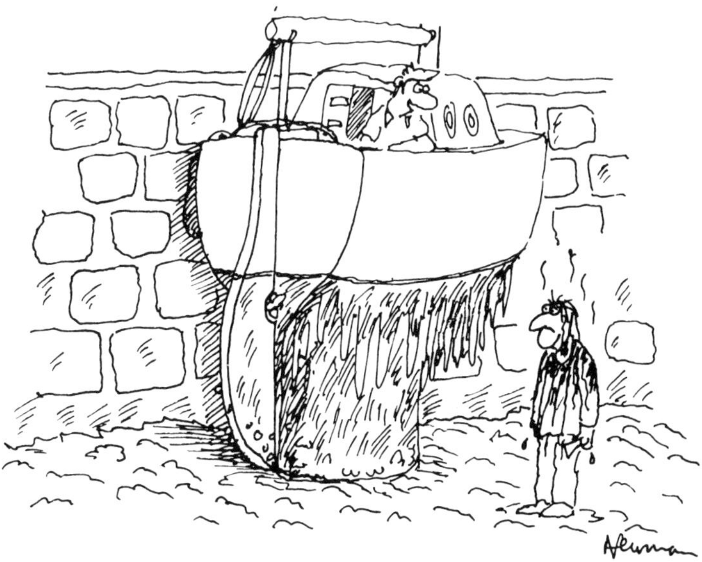

*'Great news – I've unblocked the Baby Blake!'*

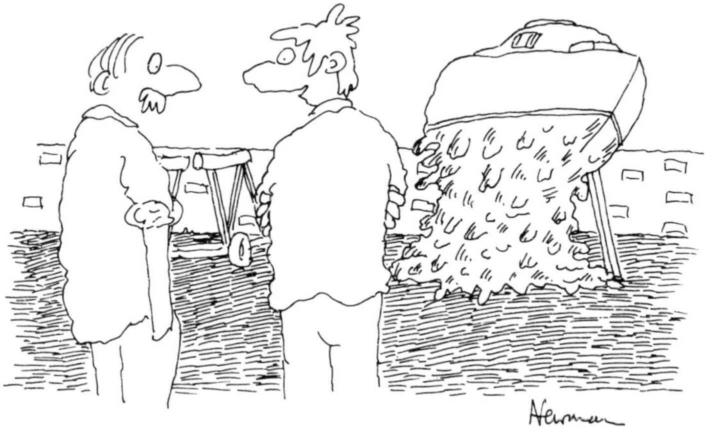

*'Somehow I don't think he'll try and burn off on GRP again . . .'*

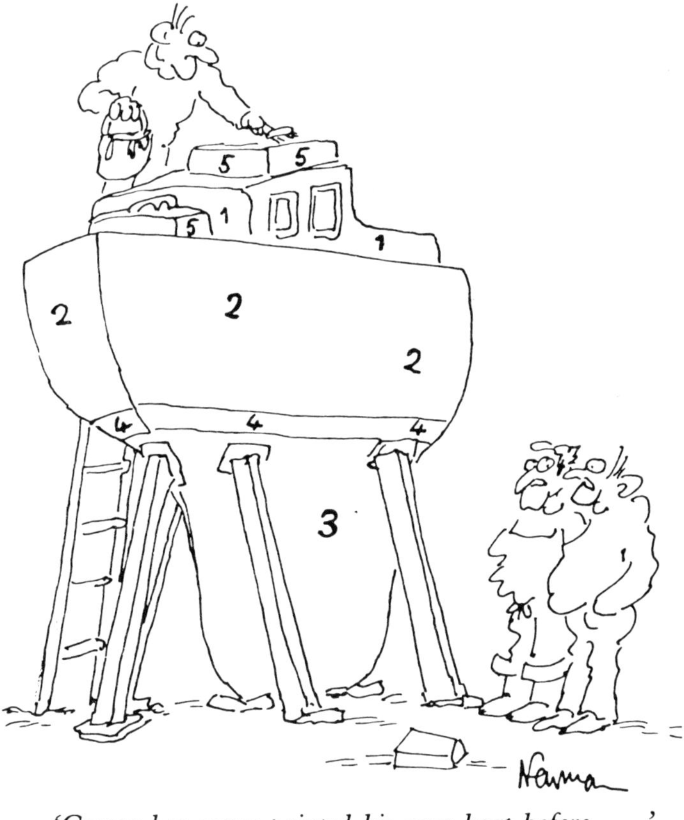


*'George has never painted his own boat before . . .'*

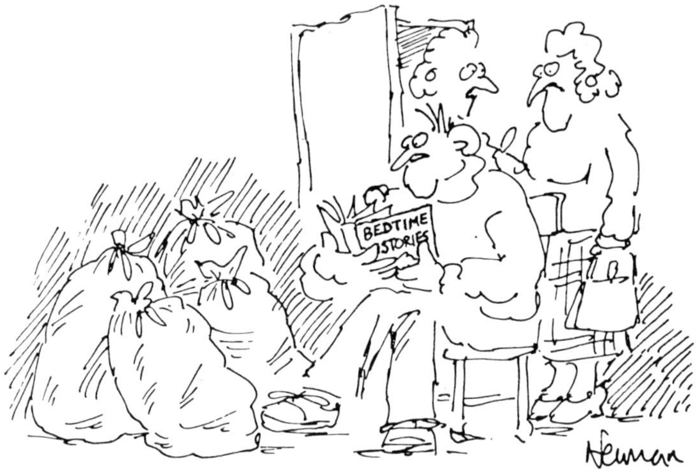


*'He takes sail care very seriously . . .'*

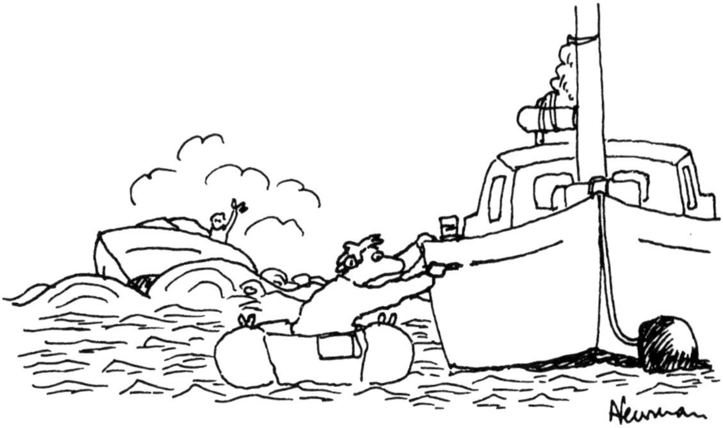

*'. . . almost finished . . .'*

# CHARTWORKMANSHIP

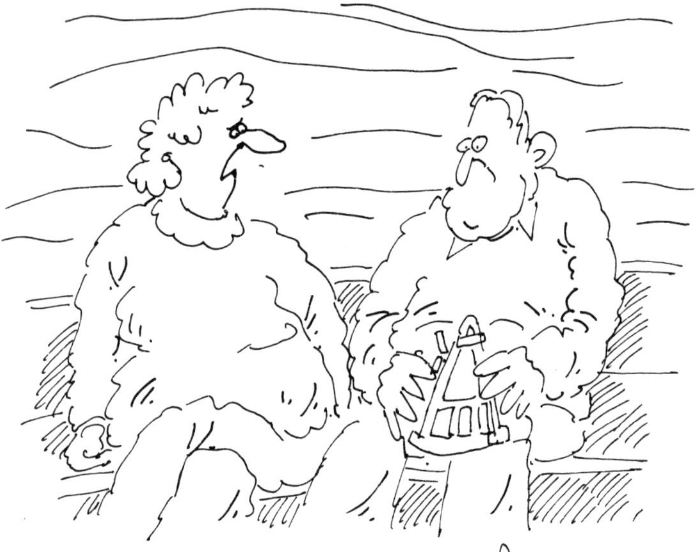


*'We haven't had a day of sunshine since you bought that damn sextant . . .'*

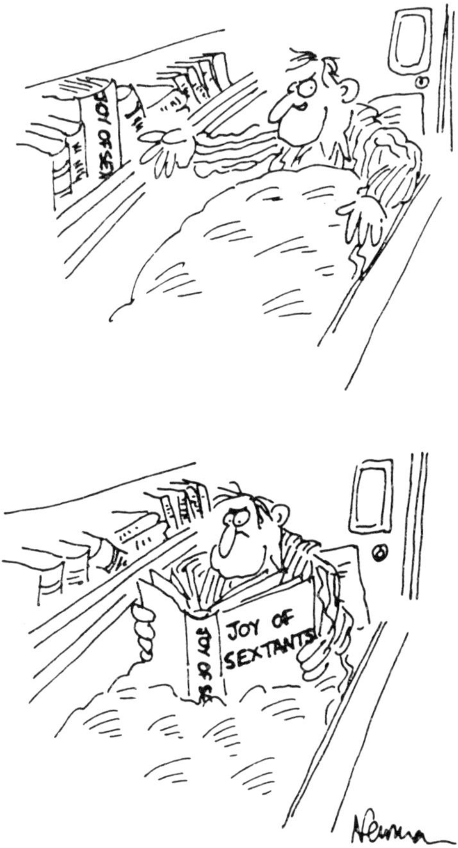
JOY OF SEX
JOY OF
SEXTANTS

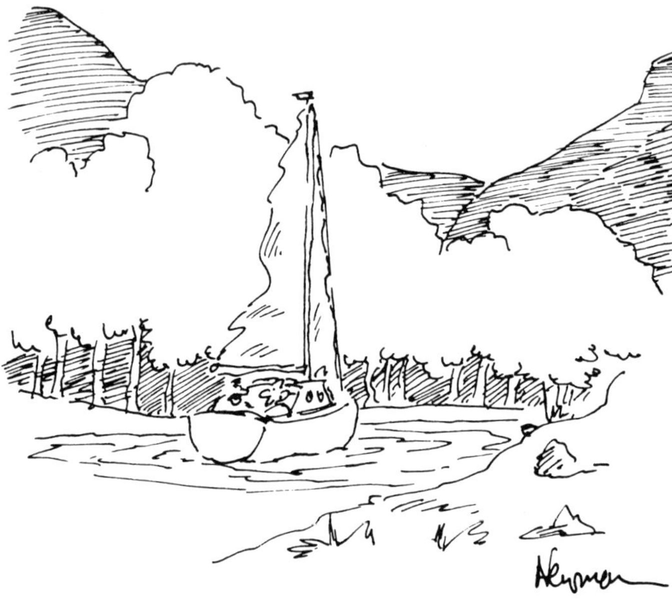

*'Well it* looked *like the bloody Alderney race when we started . . .'*

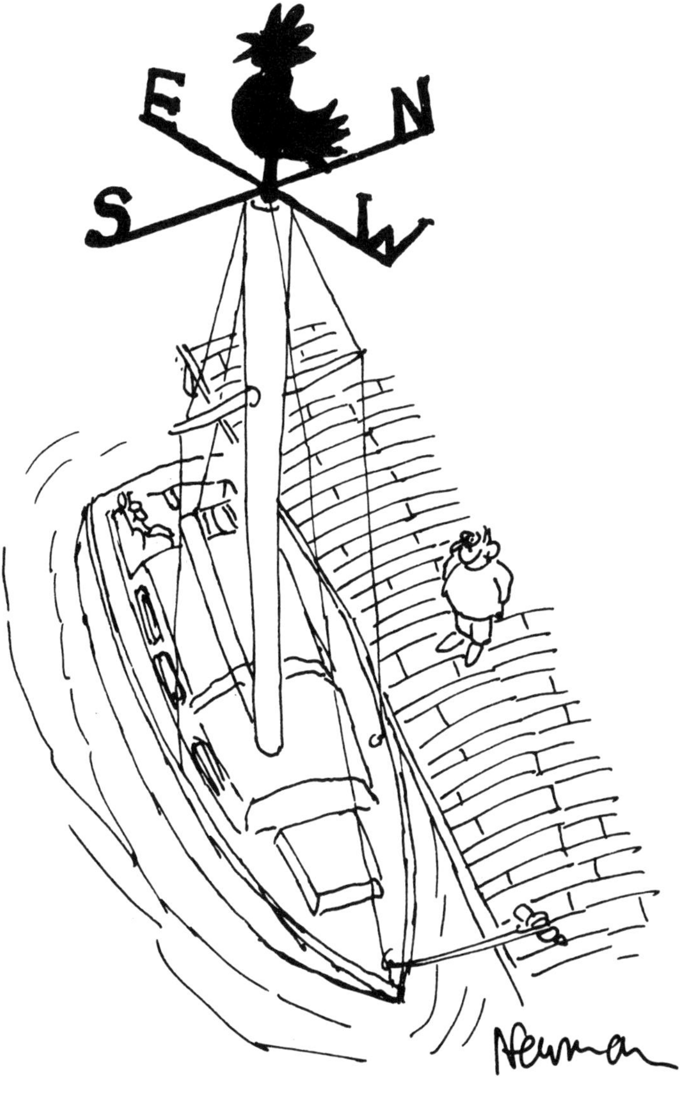
E
N
S
W

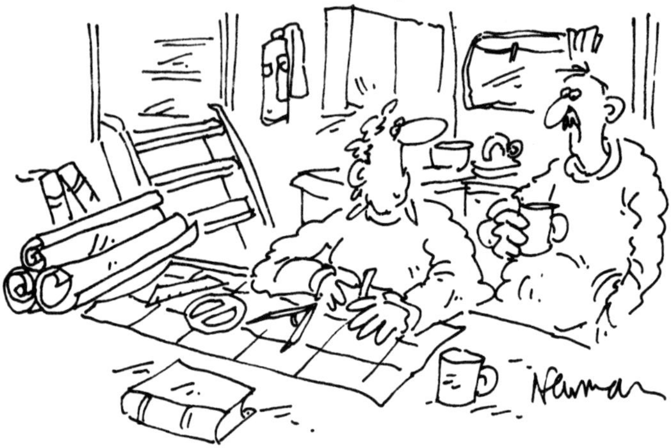


*'The Skipper says I've navigated us up Shit Creek – but I'm damned if I can find it on the chart . . .'*

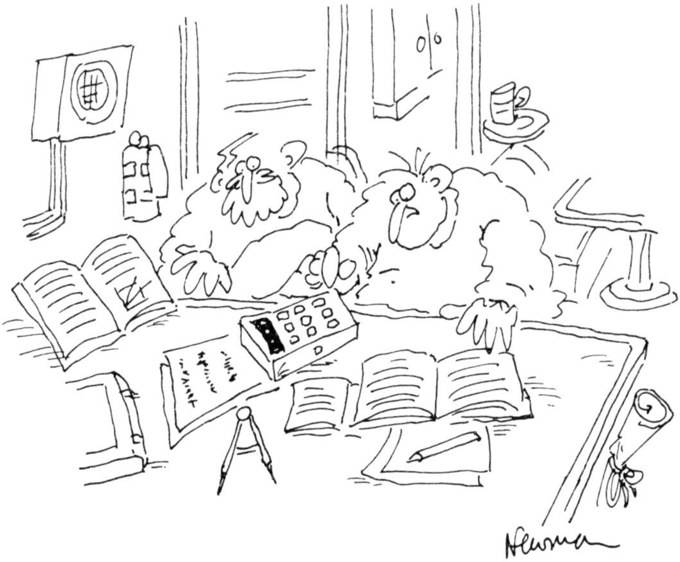


*'. . . and a simple calculation tells you* exactly *where you are. Then you just have to work out what the hell you're doing there . . .'*

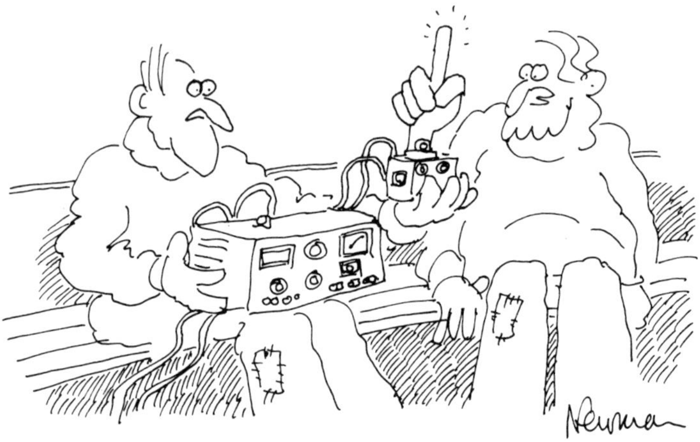


*'It's the latest thing in electronic wind direction indicators . . .'*

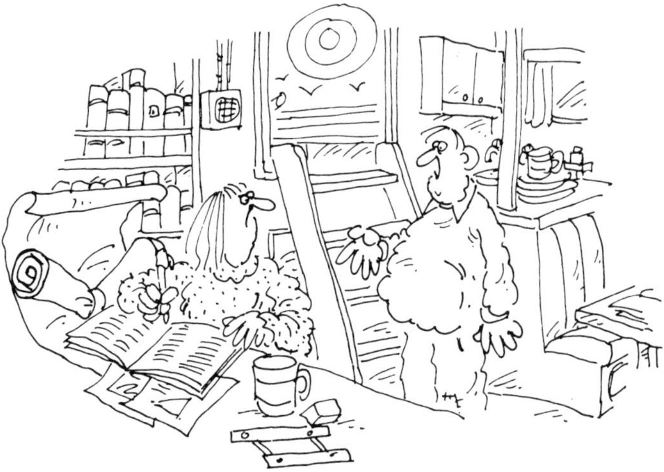

*'I'm* not *being sexist – I just don't think you should navigate by the* Cosmopolitan *horoscope.'*

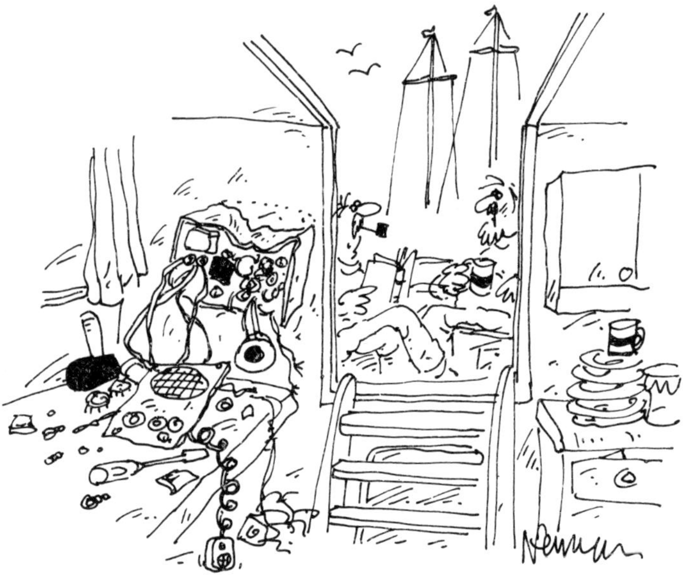

*'I'm afraid I had a little difficulty picking up the shipping forecast . . .'*

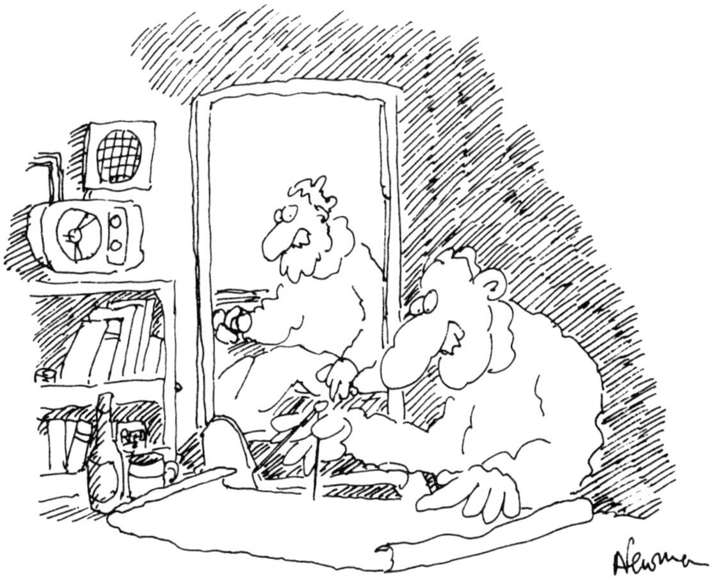

*'Well, according to my calculations we're somewhere between the ketchup bottle and the mug of coffee . . .'*

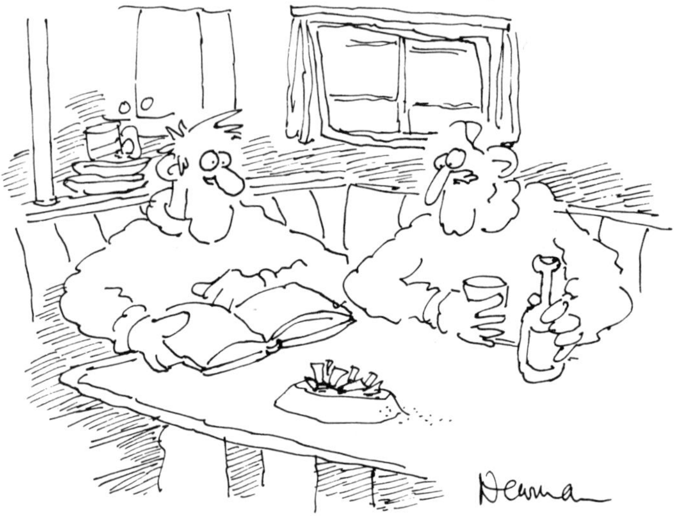

*'I bought this book on* Navigation by the Stars . . .
*It's got chapters by Bruce Forsyth, Jimmy Tarbuck, Larry Grayson . . .'*

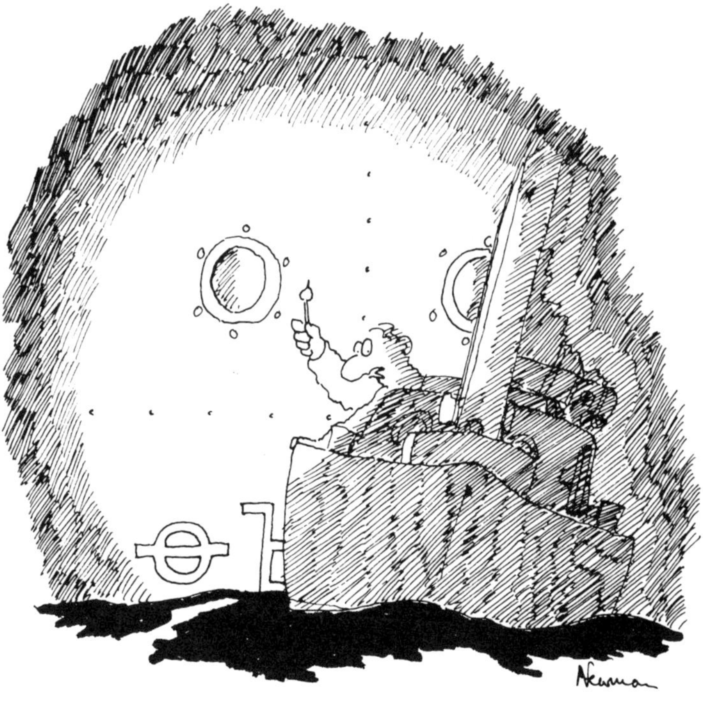

*'Well, if we* are *clear of the shipping lanes it's a very low aircraft . . .'*

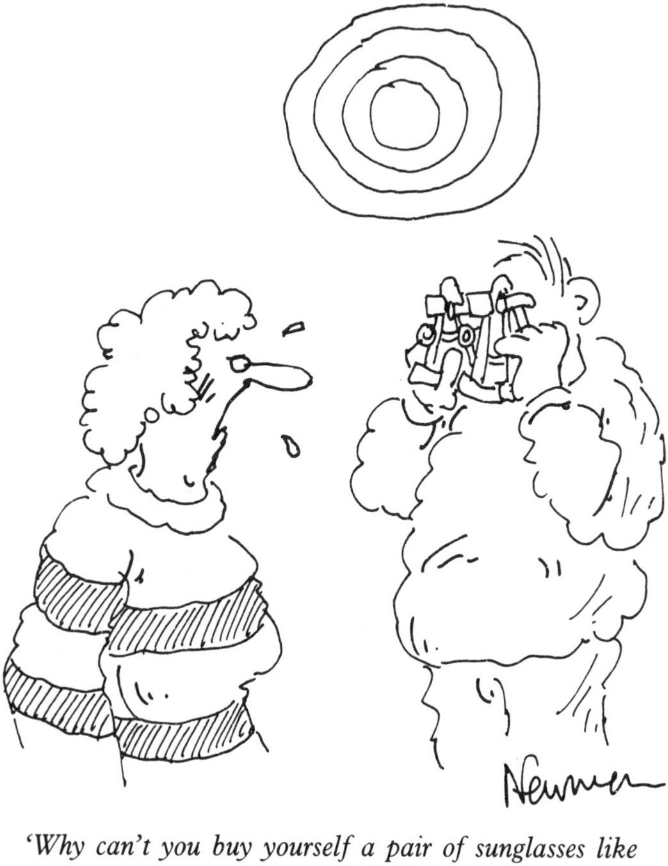


*'Why can't you buy yourself a pair of sunglasses like everyone else?'*

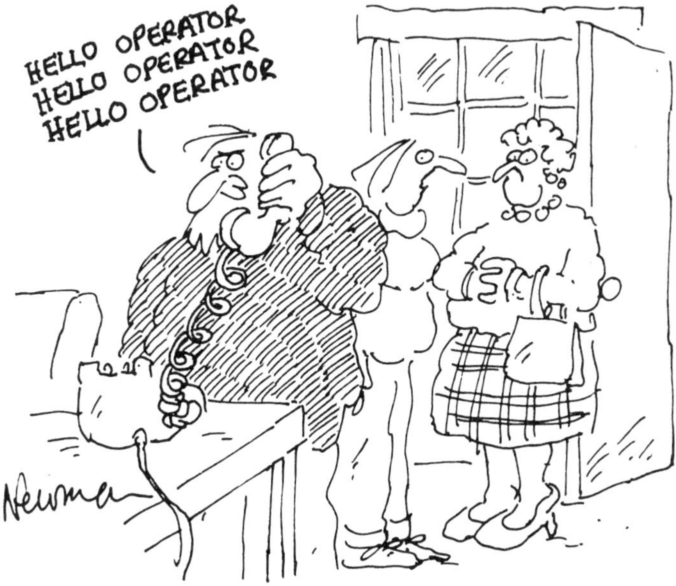


*'I think he's been at sea for too long . . .'*

# SPORTSMANSHIP

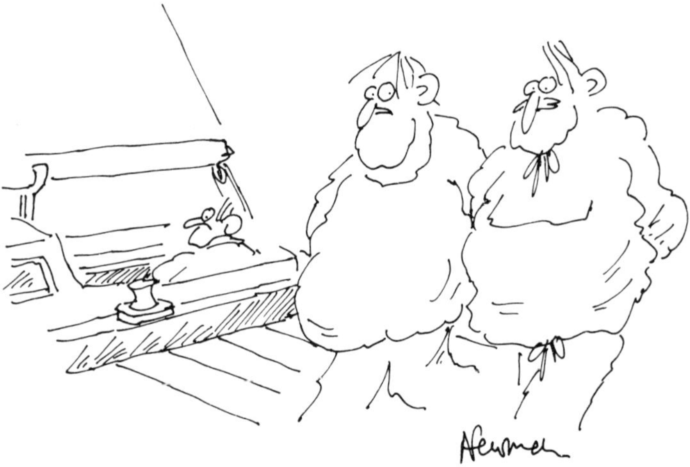

*'He took up single-handed sailing when he came back from Iran . . .'*

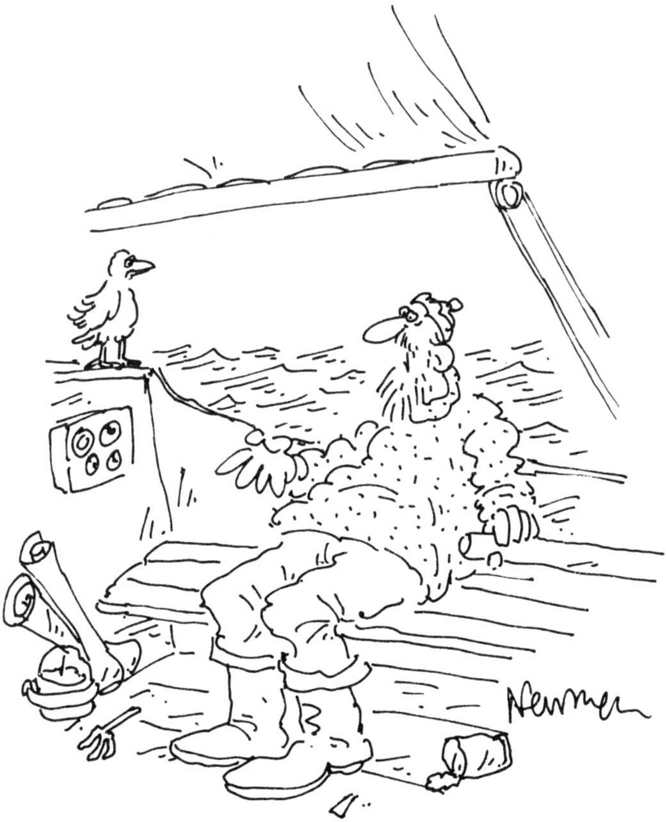

*'Of course, they all said I must be* mad *to sail the Atlantic singlehanded.'*

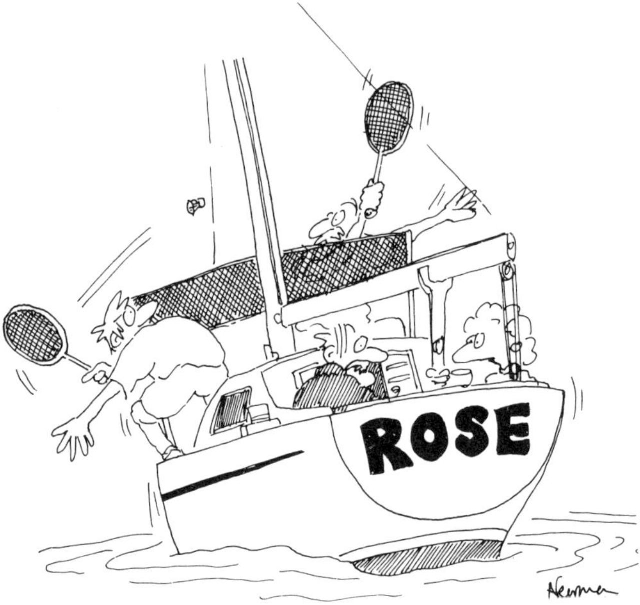


*'I've nothing against the idea, but I wonder if she's just too small for deck games . . .'*

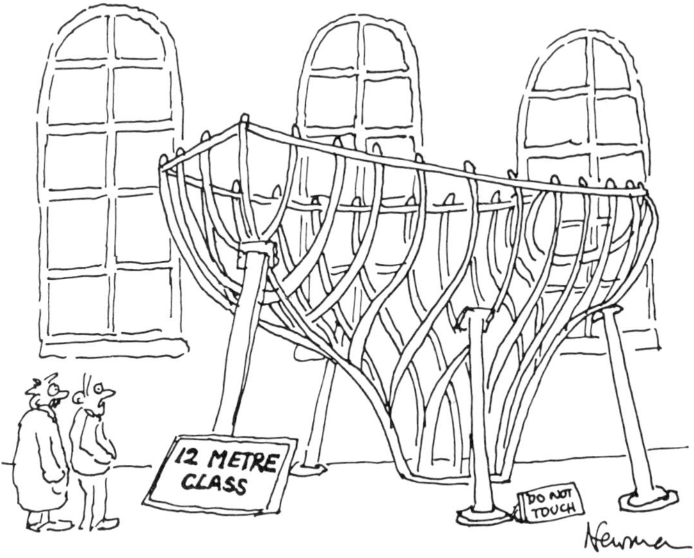


*'They say they inhabited the water to bear the enormous weight . . .'*

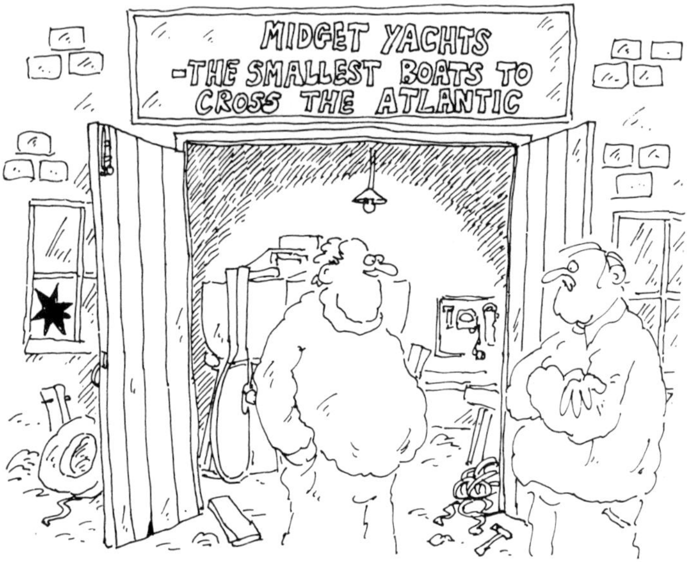


*'Business is going so well I'm thinking of moving into smaller premises . . .'*

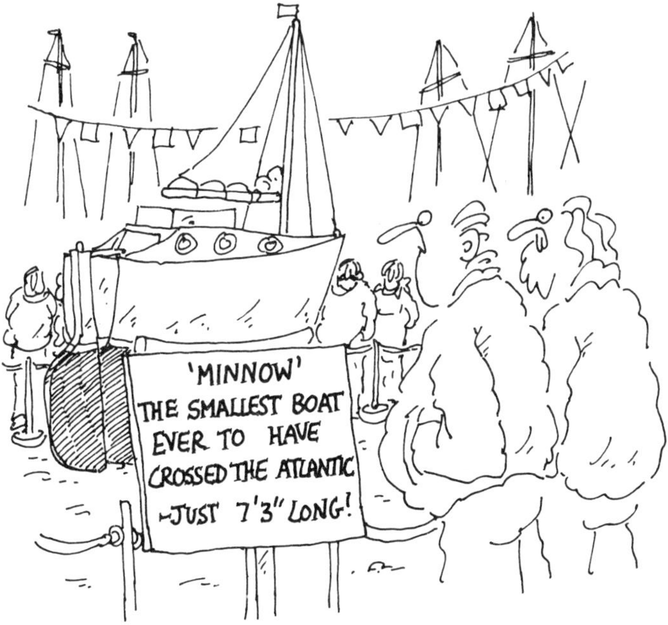


*'It could have been even shorter had he been prepared to saw off two feet . . .'*

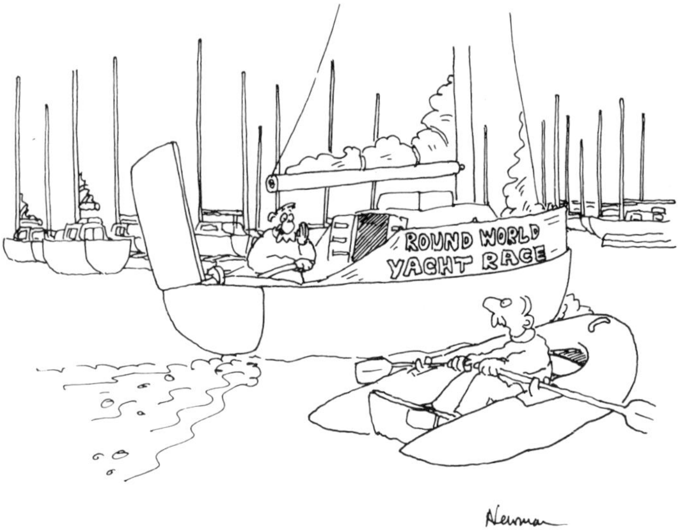


*'For God's sake! – Do I turn left or right out of the marina?'*

# WOMANSHIP

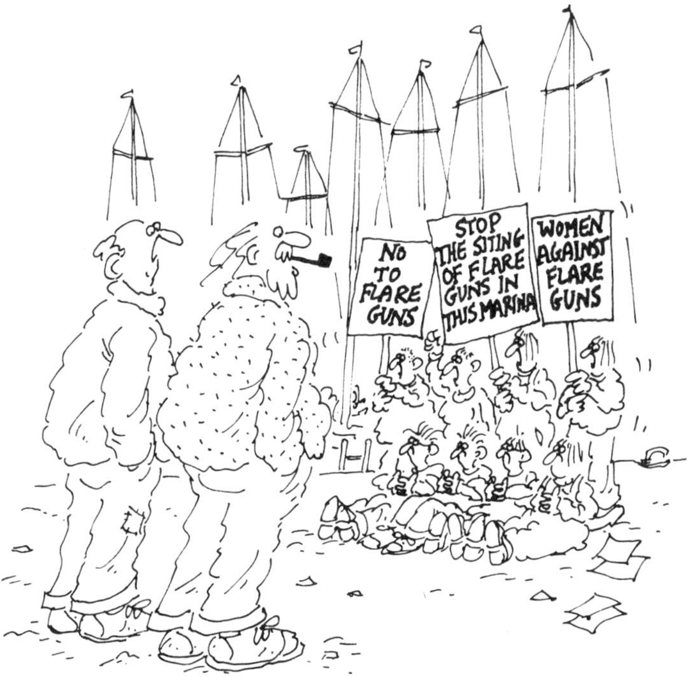


*'Oho – looks like trouble!'*

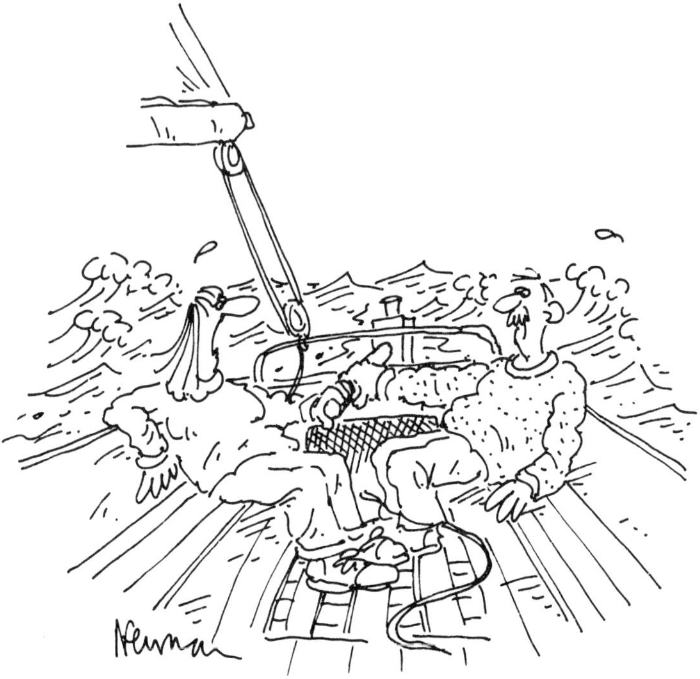

*'Let's face it, Harry, you're a pretty half-hearted feminist, aren't you?'*

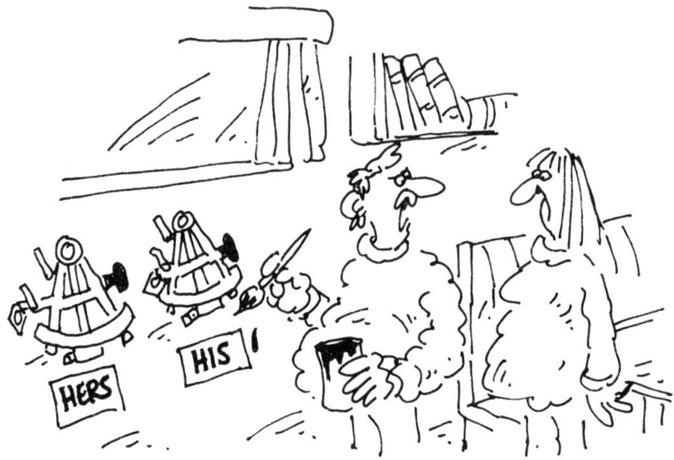


*'No-one's going to accuse me of being sextantist!'*

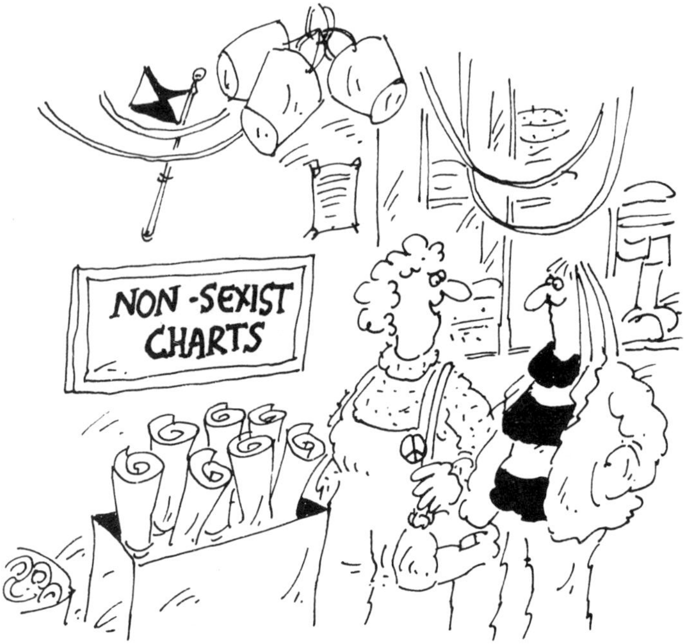


*'They have girls as well as buoys.'*

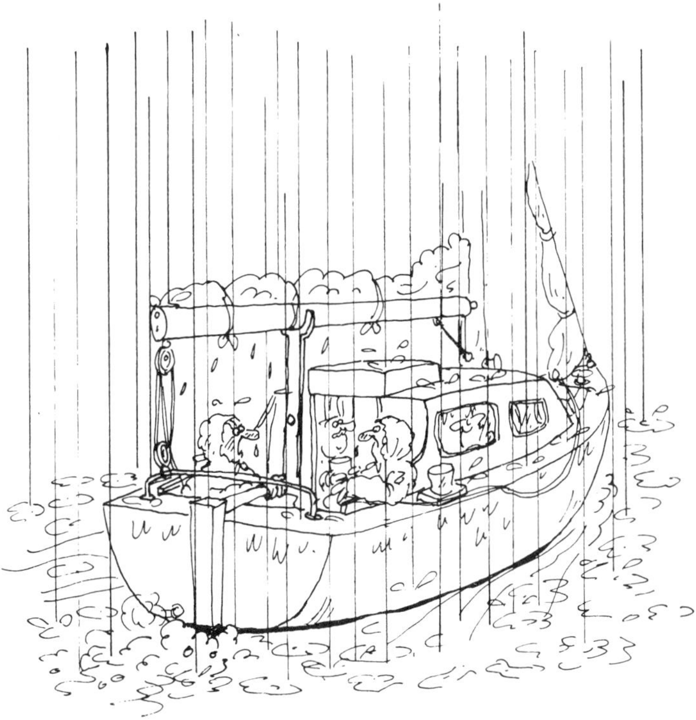

*'It's amazing when men's latent feminism surfaces!'*

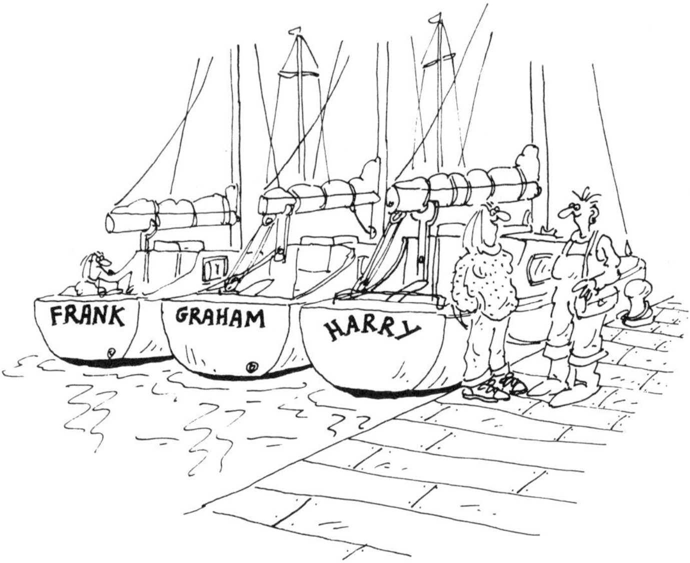


*'We're one of the least sexist marinas on the South Coast.'*

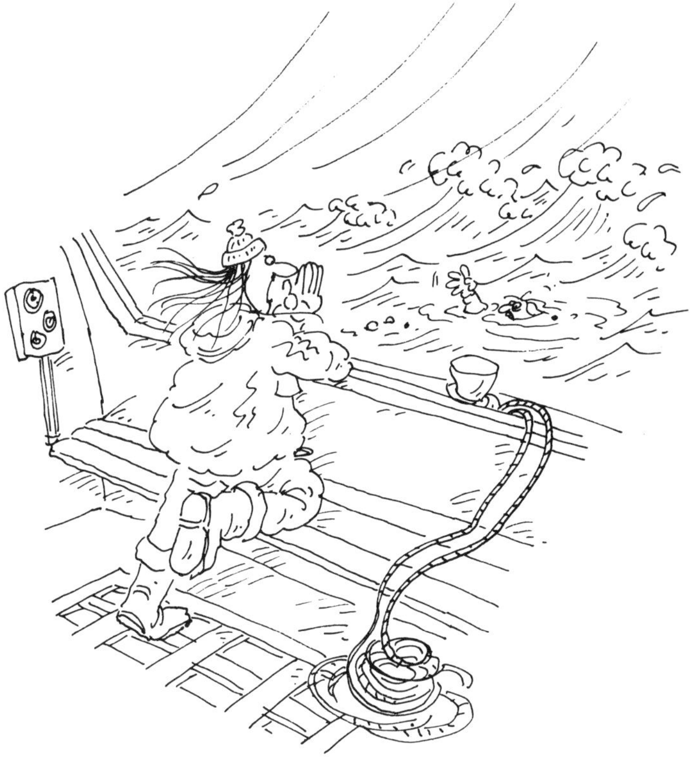

*'I'm sorry, but on ideological grounds I simply can't bring myself to shout "man overboard!"'*

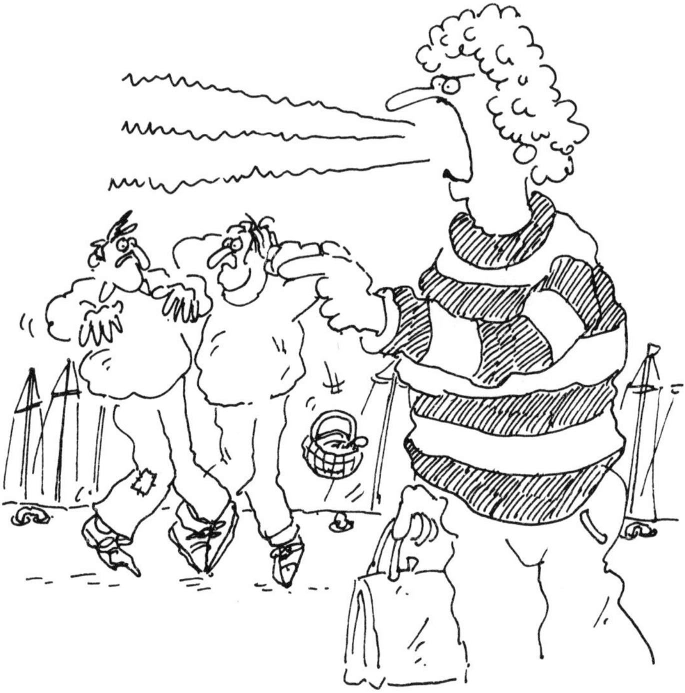

*'Who needs a radio when you've got a VHF wife?'*

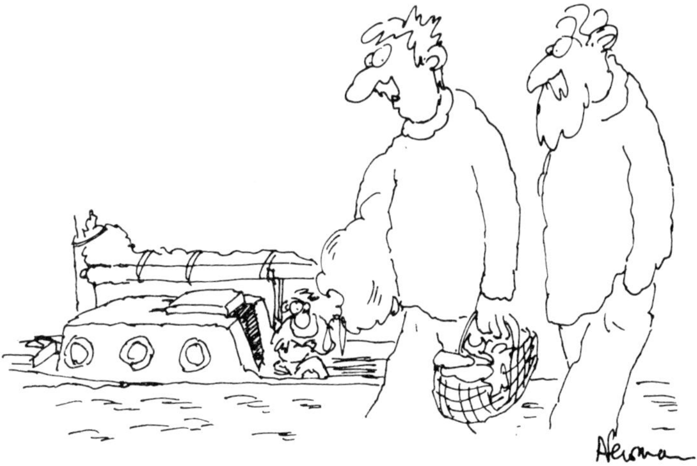

*'Harry lost his voice telling his wife he doesn't shout at her . . .'*

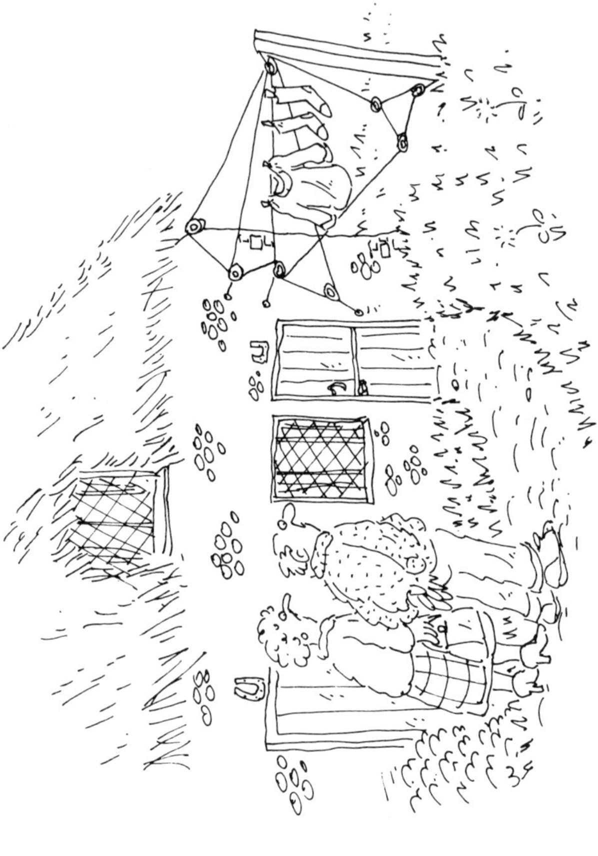

*'You can always spot an authentic old gaffer . . .'*

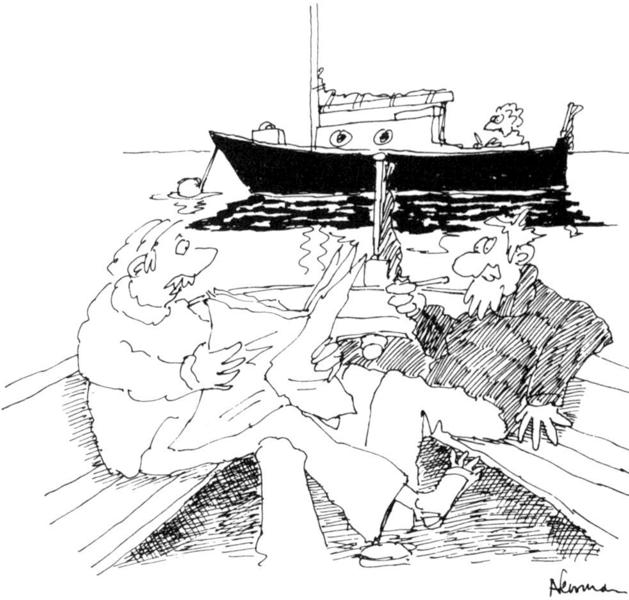

*'. . . she's ugly, noisy, expensive, handles like a pig – and his boat's not much better, either . . .'*

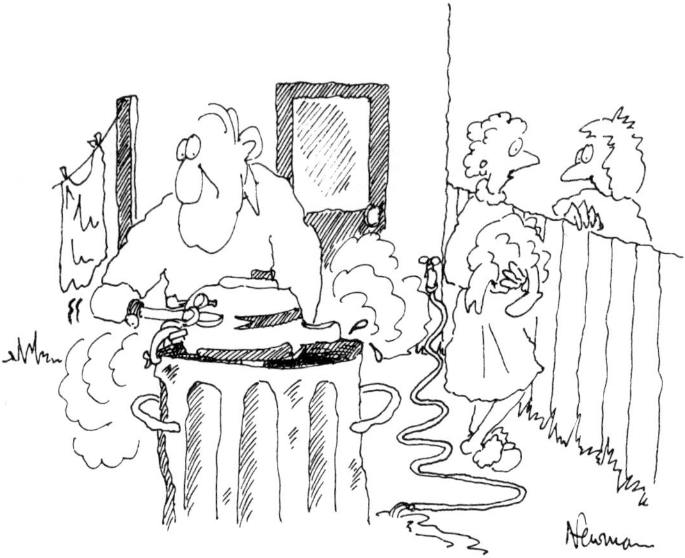

*'We don't have dustbins in this household – we have outboard motor test-beds . . .'*

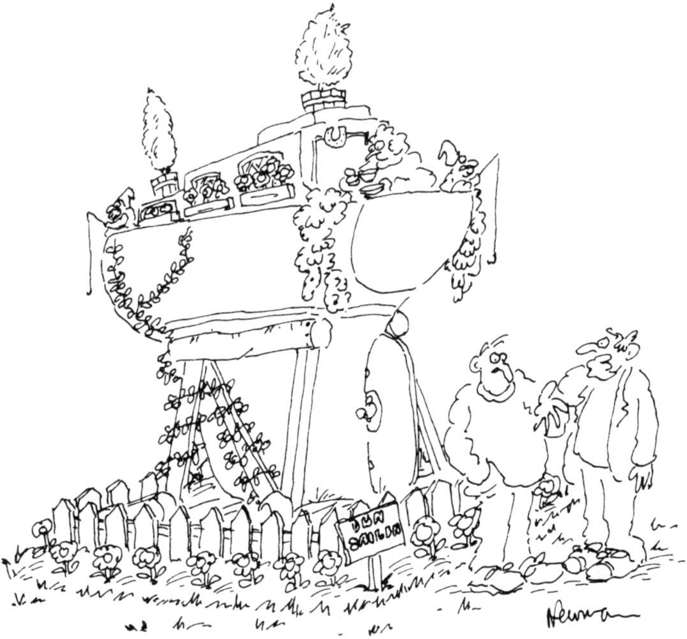

*'It was a question of compromise. I wanted a boat, and she wanted a cottage in the country.'*

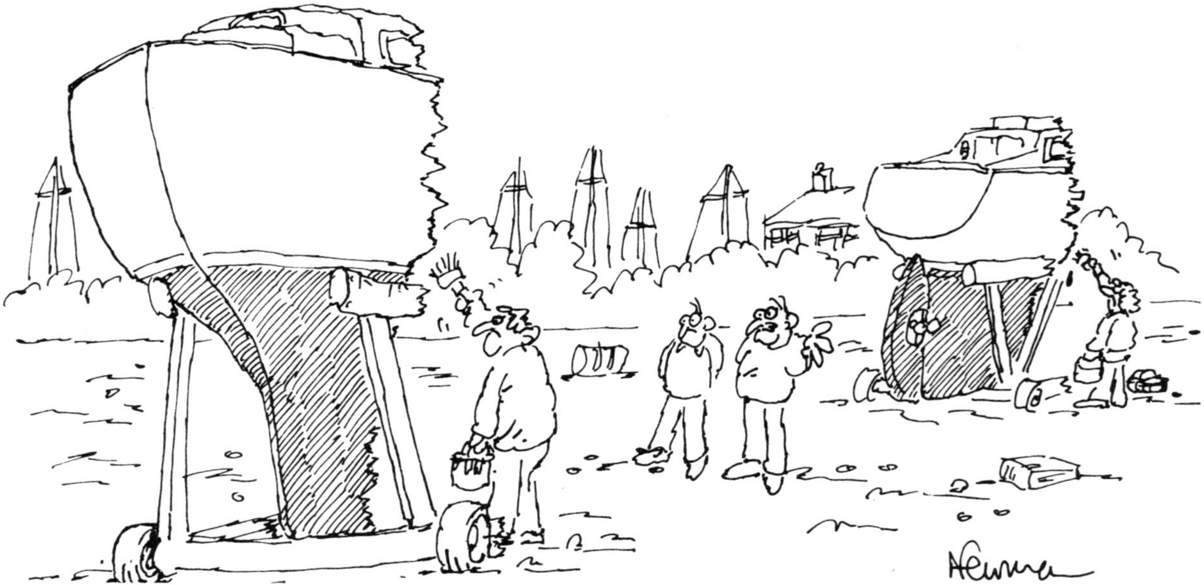

*'It was fine until they came to decide what colour to paint her . . .'*

# ONE-UPMANSHIP

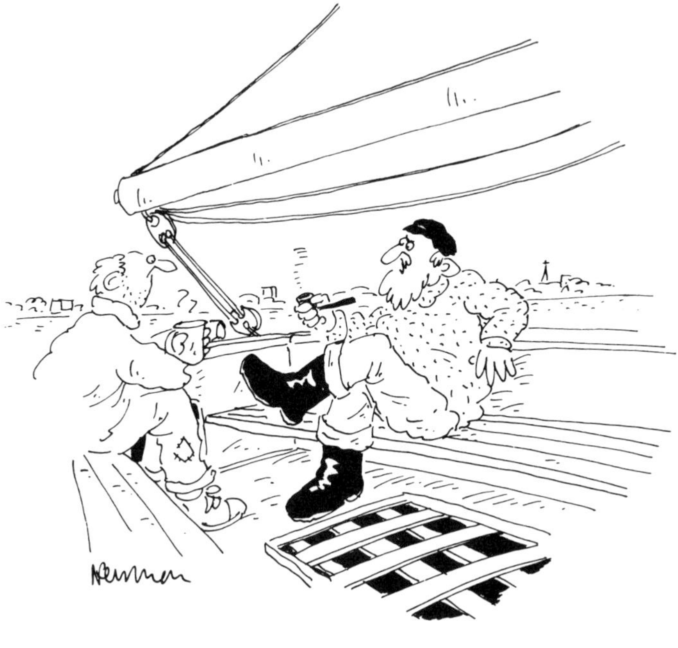

*'That was a wild night. Force 10 in the Swin and the FT index down 8 points.'*

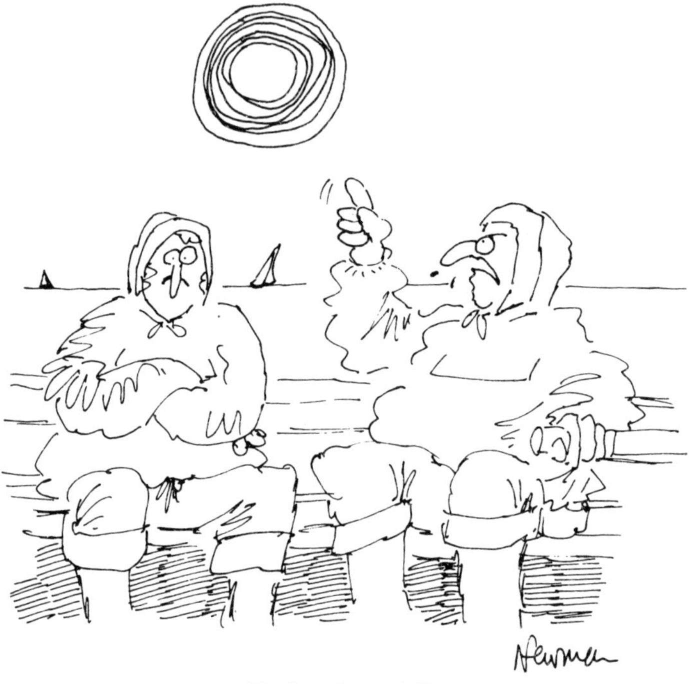


*'Rain, dammit!'*

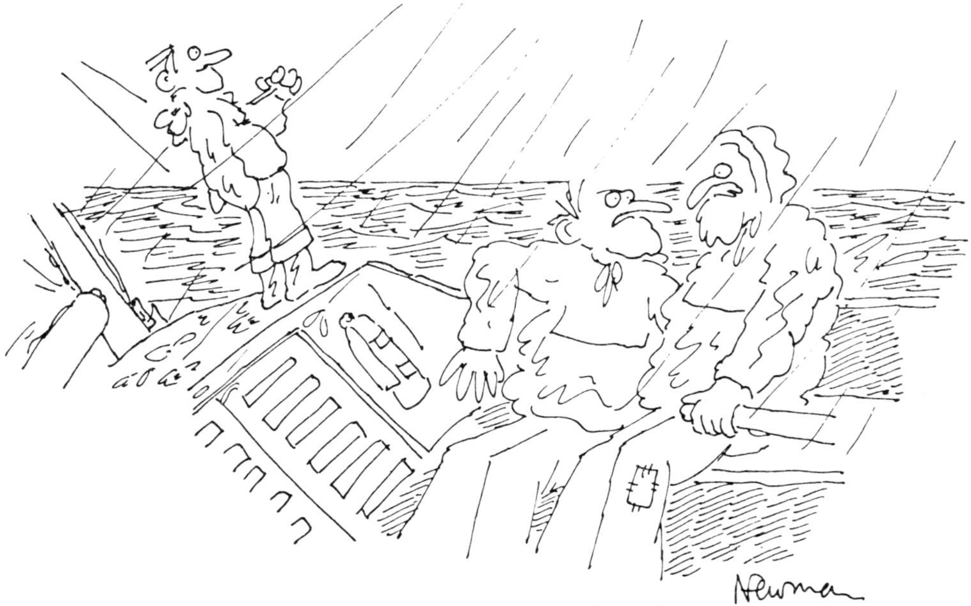

*'I wish he'd give over about those damn non-slip boots of his . . .'*

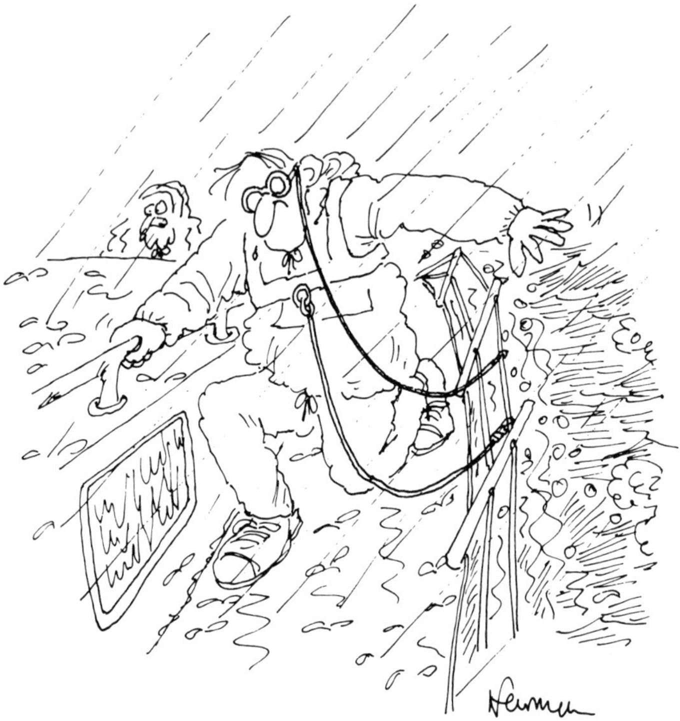
Heuman

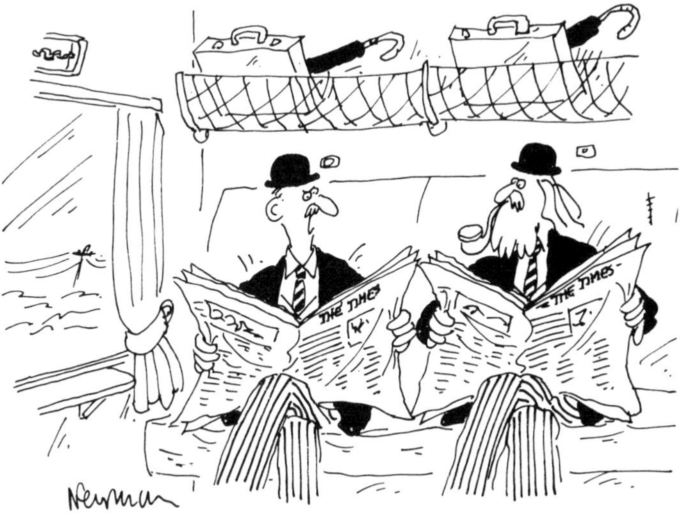


*'Aren't you taking this gaffing business a bit too far, Fenton?'*

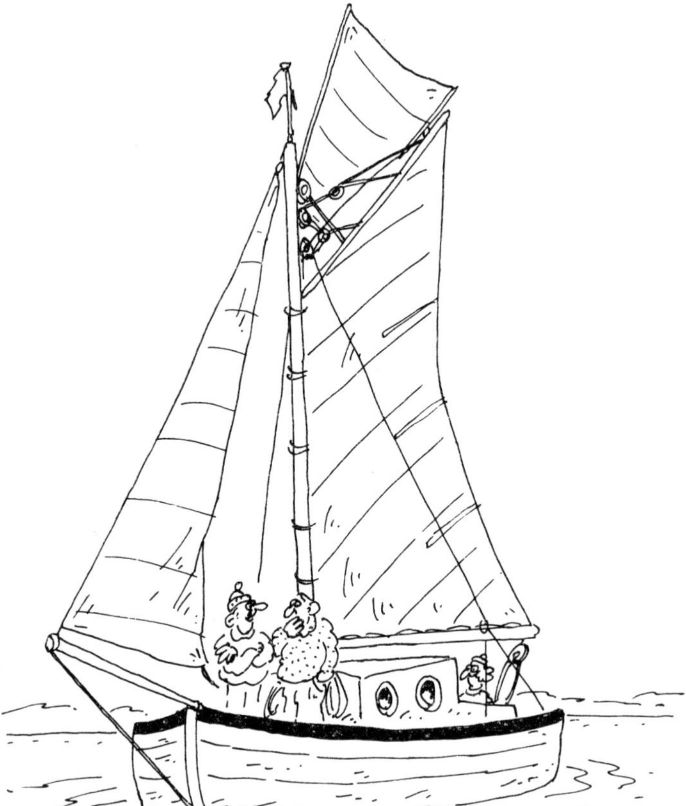

*'Timber hull, real rope, the original sails – and she's got authentic gribble worm in her deadwood.'*

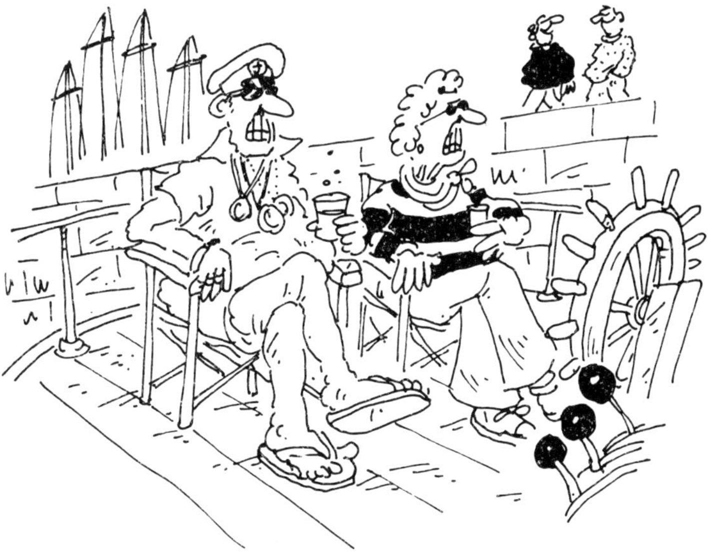

*'His varnish is peeling – and his woodwork doesn't look too good, either!'*

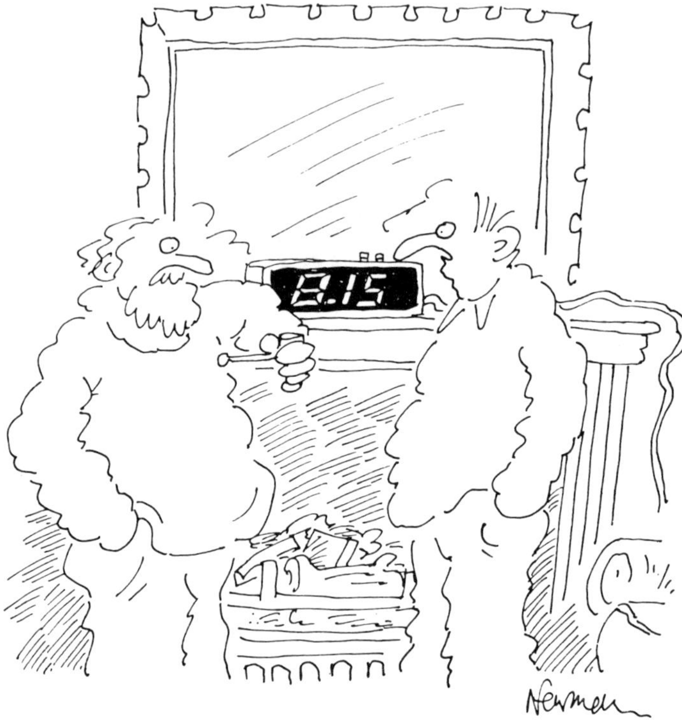


*'Somehow there isn't much mystique about a ship's digital clock on your mantlepiece . . .'*

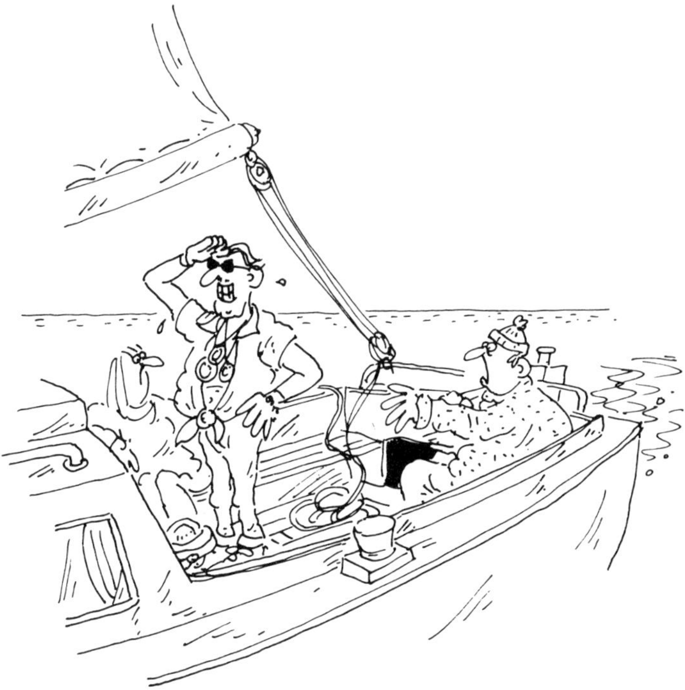

*'For God's sake don't let him stand near the compass!'*

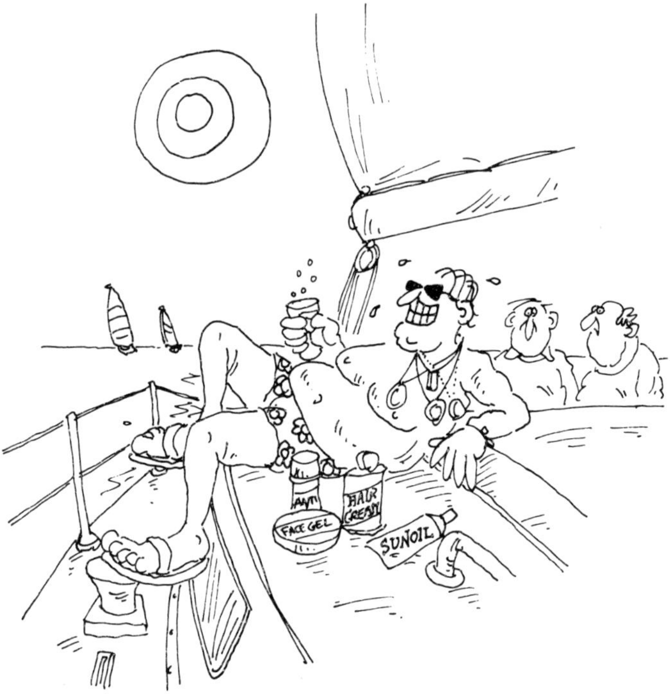


*'At least with him on board we don't need a radar reflector.'*

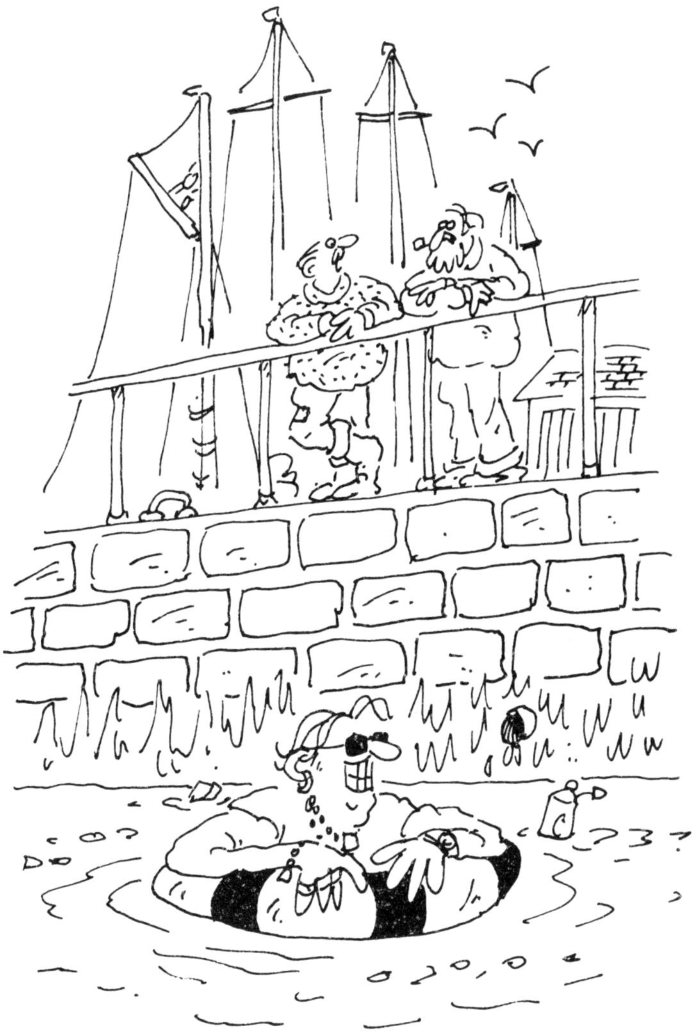

*'Don't worry – he hasn't fallen overboard. He's just getting his jeans skin-tight.'*

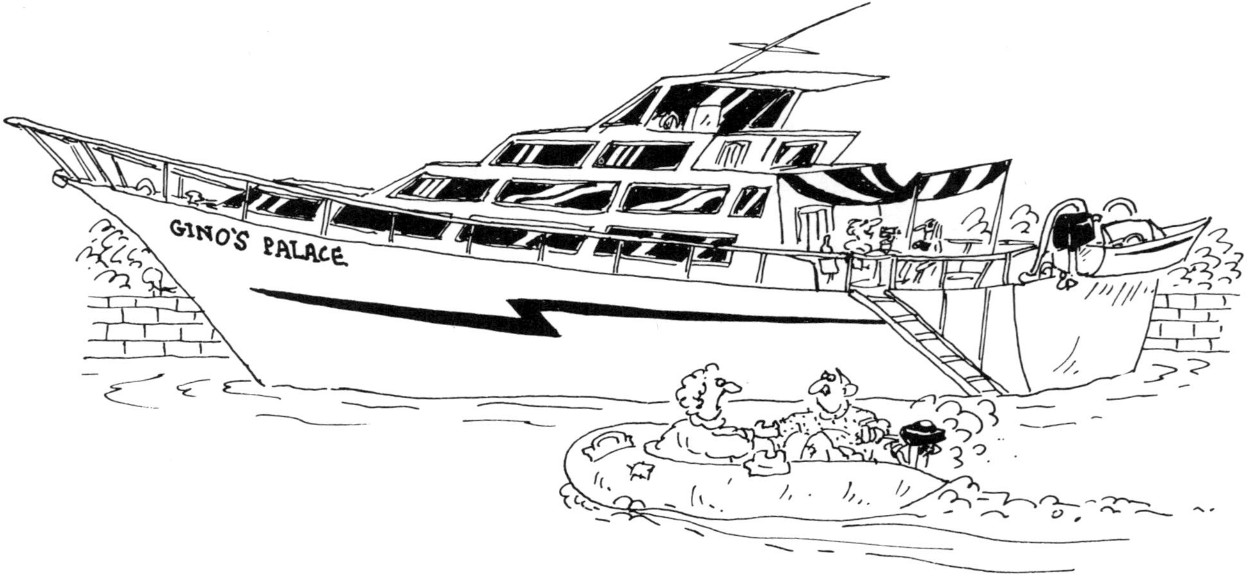


*'If it's only a symbol of sexual inadequacy, why isn't the reverse true?'*

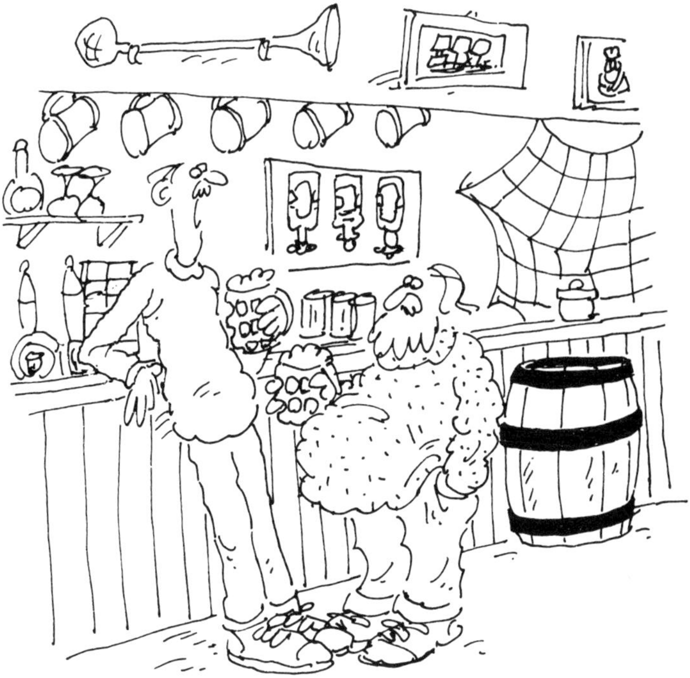

*'You see, that's the difference between us Bermudan riggers and you gaffers. You have such poor aspect ratio.'*

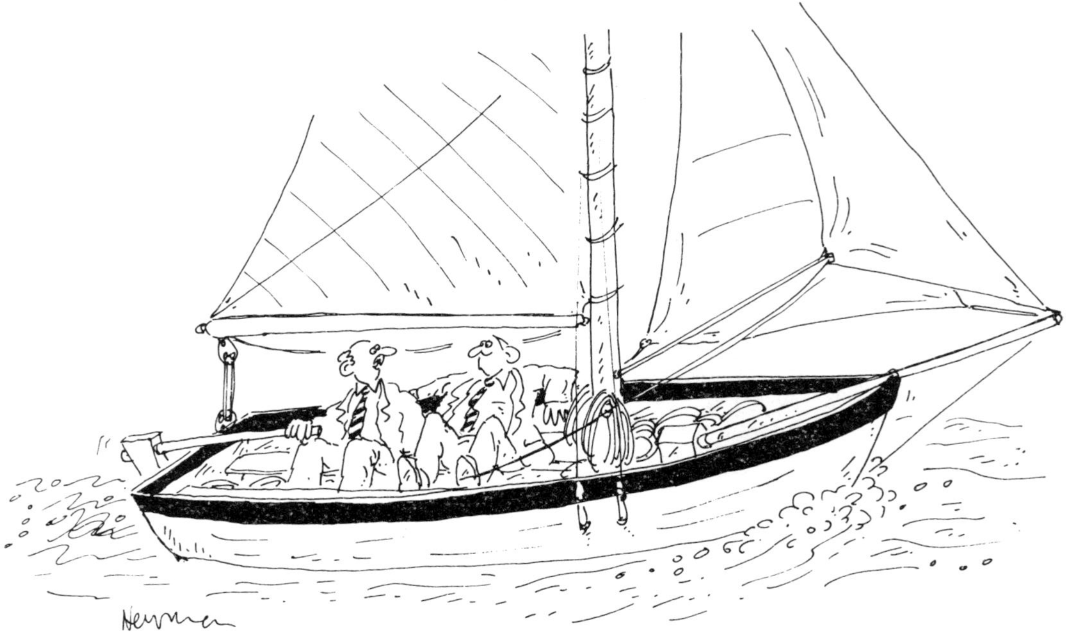

*'Absolutely* everything's *authentic, old boy!'*

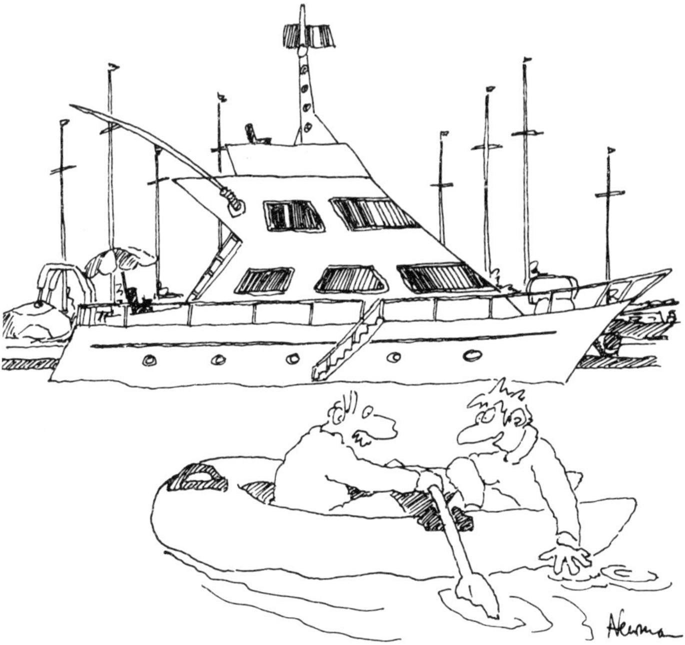

*'Don't tell anyone – it's a pedalo . . .'*

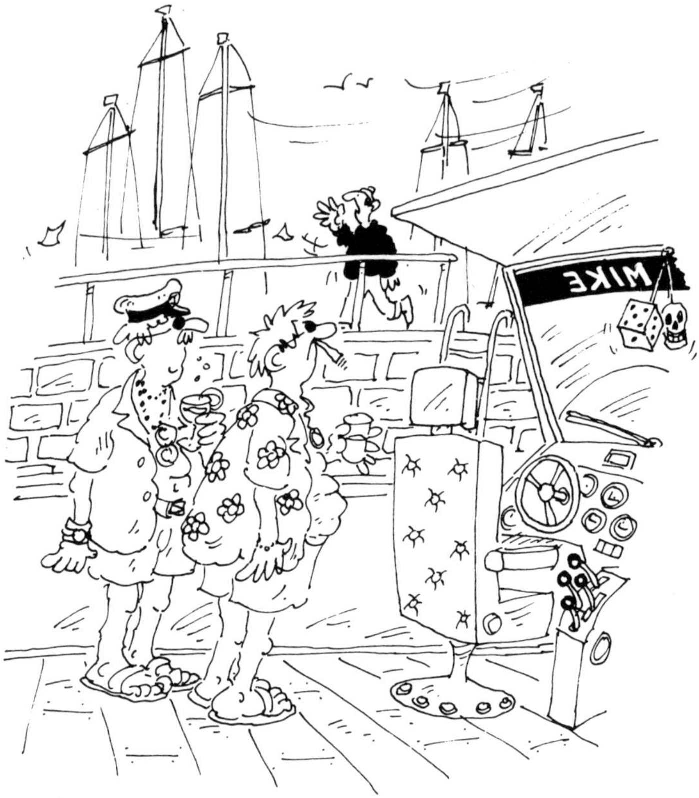

*'Force 10 blowing up! Batten down the hatches!*
*Nail down the toupées!'*

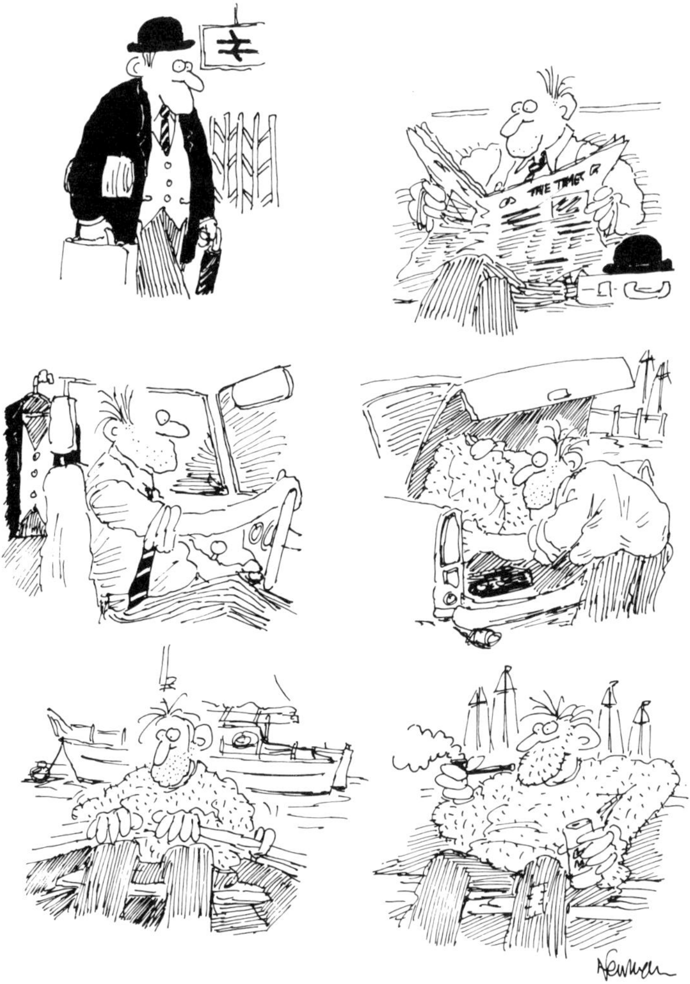
THE TIMES

# SALESMANSHIP

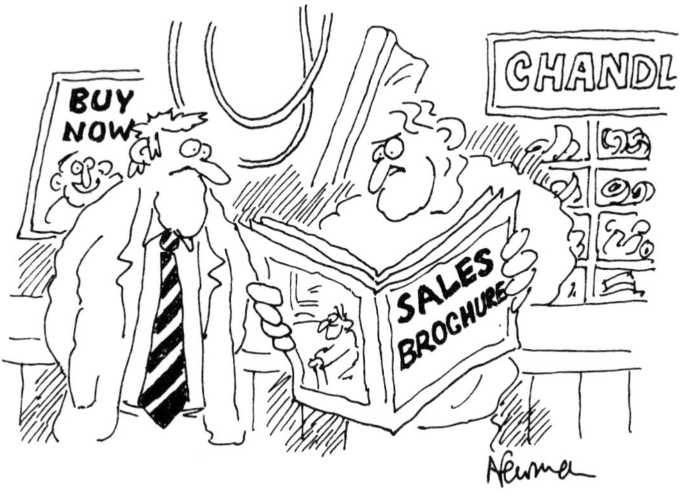


*'It's just as well they're single-handed systems – they cost you an arm and a leg to buy them . . .'*

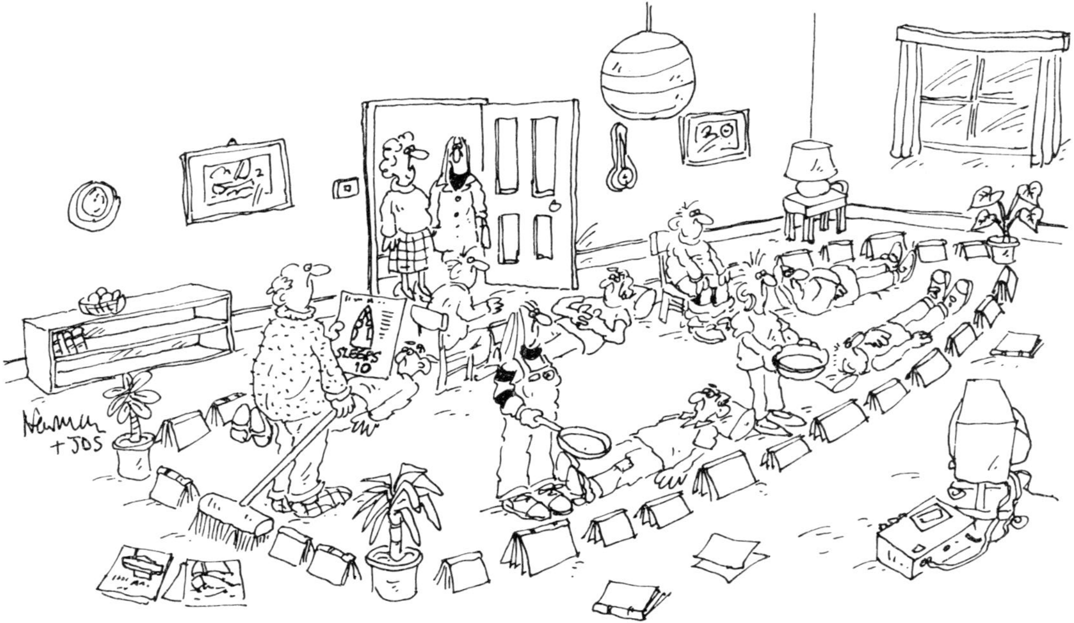


*'Dad doesn't believe the brochure.'*

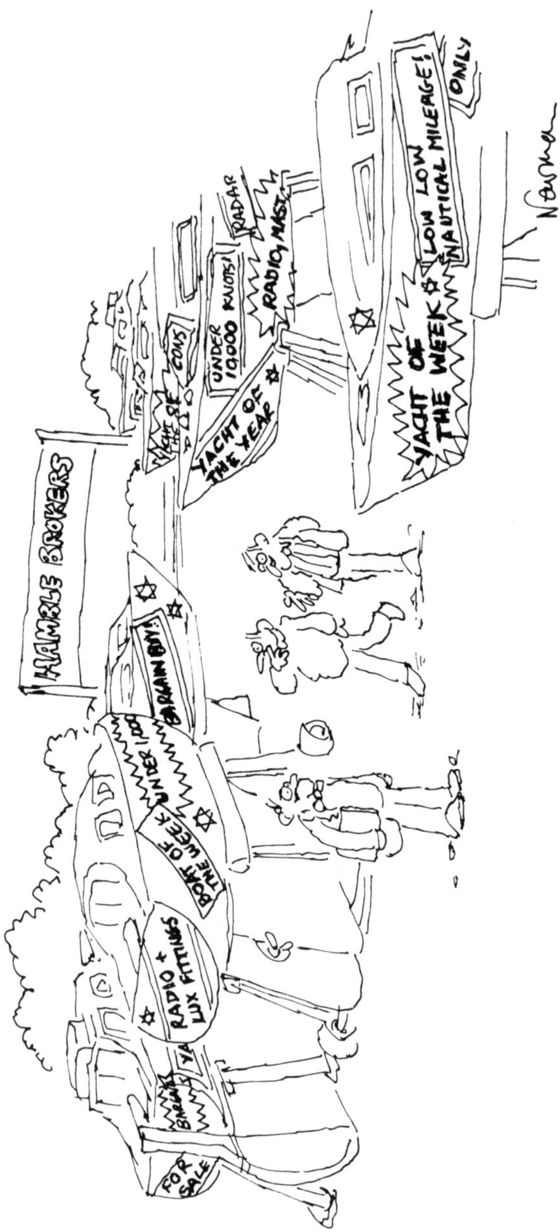


*'Ron here used to be a second-hand car salesman . . .'*

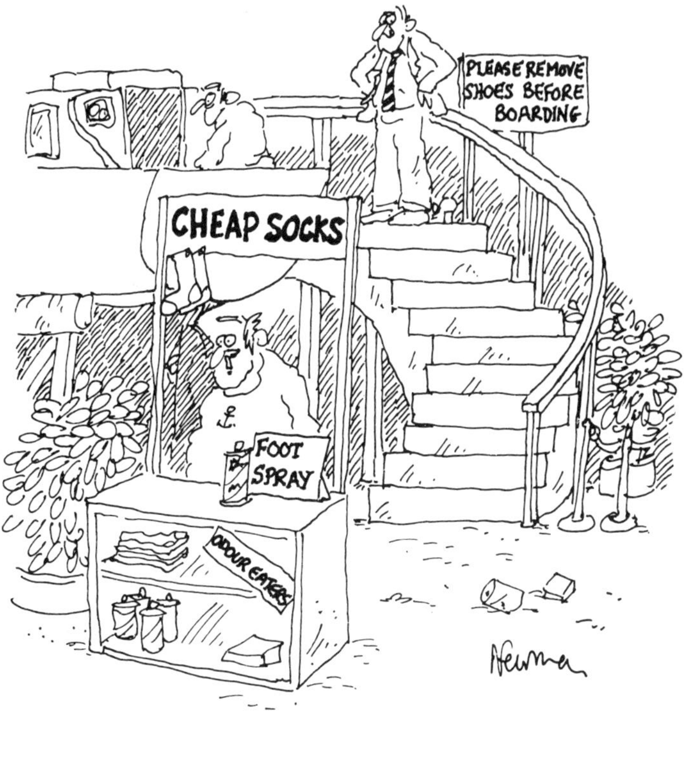
PLEASE REMOVE SHOES BEFORE BOARDING
CHEAP SOCKS
FOOT SPRAY
ODOUR EATERS
Newman

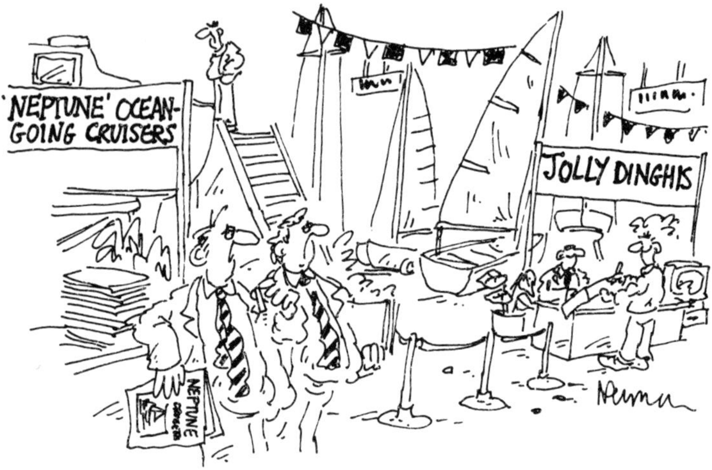


*'If there's one thing I can't stand, it's people with more sense than money . . .'*

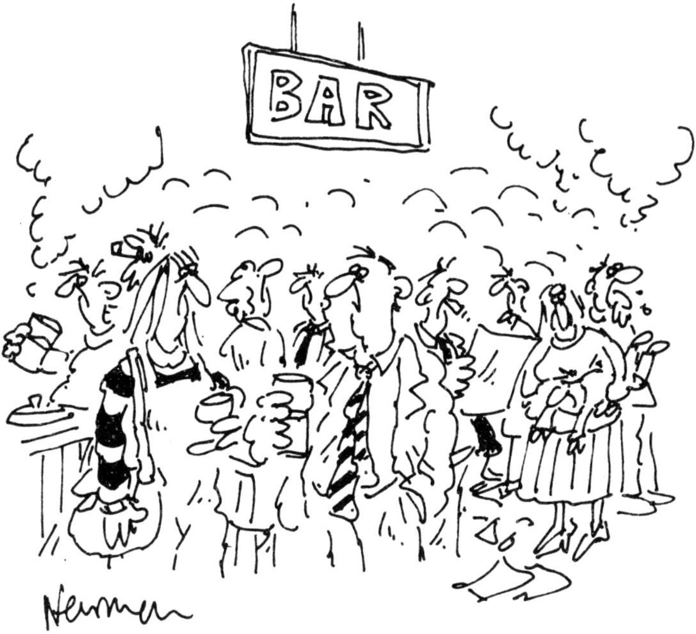


*'For goodness sake, don't judge sailing by the Boat Show. Sailing's far worse.'*

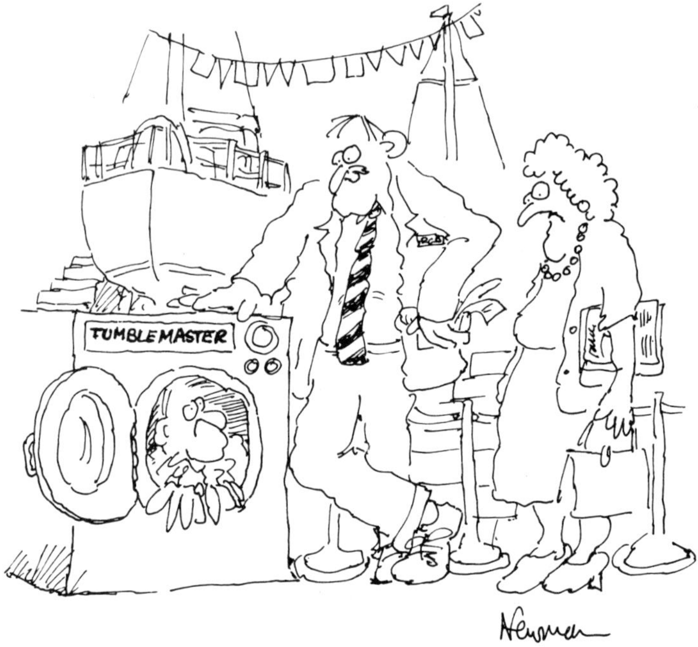


*'I think this'll give you the feel of it, sir . . .'*